DO NOT SAY, I AM TOO YOUNG

by
Dominic Russo

Harrison House

Tulsa, OK

15 14 13 12 11 10   10 9 8 7 6 5 4 3 2 1

Do Not Say, I Am Too Young
ISBN 978-160683-191-5
ISBN 1-60683-191-7

Copyright © 2010 by
Dominic Russo
Rochester, MI 48306

Published by Harrison House Publishers
P.O. Box 35035
Tulsa, OK 74153
www.harrisonhouse.com

Harrison House

DEDICATION

I dedicate these pages first to my Lord Jesus. I cried out to You in prayer, and you heard me and gave me all the desires of my heart. All my days are Yours.

I dedicate this book to my amazing parents - the two most godly people on the face of the earth. Dad and Mom, thank you for paying the price and paving the way.

I dedicate this book to all my mentors and heroes. John and Lisa Bevere, Peter and Anne Pretorius, Pastor Dennis Slavens, Dr. Myles Munroe, Ron Luce, Bob Harrison, Dr. T. L. Osborn, the late Pastor Billy Joe Daugherty and the late Dr. Oral Roberts.

I dedicate this book to the DRM team, the people that make "going to work" too good to be true. Mrs. "T", Libby, Matt, Rigo, Pastor Fleming - you are absolutely extraordinary.

I dedicate this book to The Gathering at OCC. You've been a huge part of my life - what a family.

I dedicate this book to my best friends: Gabe, Matt, Cooper, Chris, Jesse, J-Rus - I pray we run together for the rest of our lives.

I lastly dedicate this book to my beautiful wife, Lindsay. Babe, we both know this project would still be half finished, saved in a Word document if it wasn't for you. Your support, encouragement, and friendship continue to exceed my wildest dreams about marriage. I still believe. I love you.

CONTENTS

FOREWORD

I believe that God is raising up a generation of young people who will respond to God's calling on their lives with passion and purpose. I'm seeing a generation of young people before us that are not hindered by what people think of them and are determined to give all they have to see people reached with the Gospel. This is why I believe Dominic's book is so important.

I've known Dominic Russo since he was fifteen years old. He is one of the most outstanding young men I know. He responded to the call of God at an early age, kept himself free from entanglements, and was able to radically pursue what God had planned for him. I have kept a keen eye on him since he was young and have watched as he has matured to the place of doing large crusades in foreign countries at a very young age. This isn't due to a 'special' calling on his life, but a willingness to hear what God is saying and respond in obedience.

Today it is so easy to get caught up in what society or peers want you to do and say, and to put off God's purpose for when you get older. The world actually encourages you to just go with the flow. And let's be honest. It actually is easier to go with culture and not buck the current system. But that isn't God's best. He has called you to be an extraordinary individual and His divine plan for your life can be revealed to you at a very early age.

I remember God's word to me about age groups. The world has four different distinct age groups: infants, children, teenagers, and adults. However, if you look in the Bible you will only see three age groups: infants, children, and adults. The Bible clearly illustrates that there is no in between age group from children to adults. That is why a young Jewish man goes through Bar Mitzvah at age 13. God then sees him as an adult and thus plans to use him as such!

I've spoken at over a thousand churches over the years and the most successful churches I've witnessed are those that treat young people not as the church of tomorrow, but as the church of today. They actively encourage the youth to serve in ministry, get involved in the worship team, and usher. These churches don't treat the youth as a separate age group, but embrace them as active members of the Body. This is how God always intended it!

I'm so excited to endorse this project by Dominic Russo because he is truly someone who has experienced firsthand how God can actively move through a young person. My hope is that as you read this book you'll open your heart and listen to the God-calling for your life. I believe that this book will deposit a seed in your heart that will grow and propel you into your divine destiny. Remember, you were created to go beyond the ordinary and live an extraordinary life!

John Bevere

Author / Speaker

Messenger International

Colorado Springs / Australia / United Kingdom

INTRODUCTION

Your story is being written. With every moment that passes and every decision that's made, another page is added to your book. This is the story of your life. I'm convinced it is not going to be a sad book, a frustrating book, or a depressing book. Your book will not disappoint; it's going to rock.

The cool thing about the story you and I are writing is that God allows us to write it. He doesn't force a plot or demand certain characters be incorporated. We get to pick the story line and the main characters.

I can't stop thinking about how we only have one shot at creating the outcome; we have one opportunity to determine the plot. Once our life on earth ends, we leave time and enter eternity. There are no "do-overs," no erasers.

I want to challenge you to live your life in a way that makes your story speak years after you have left this earth. The writer of Hebrews said, "It was by faith that Abel brought a more acceptable offering to God than Cain did... Although Abel is long dead, he still speaks to us..." (Hebrews 11:4,NLT). Abel is dead, but he is still speaking. Because of his faith, several thousand years later we can still hear him talking. His life is a story that is being told. As you absorb the pages of this book, I want you to think about your life and the story it is telling.

You and I have a huge assignment. We have to move our generation. In the U.S. alone, a monumental shift is taking place. 66% of our grandparents are Bible-believing Christians; 34% of our parents are the same. The sobering reality is that only 4% of the current generation believes the Bible is actually God's Word. In the U.S., so many young people simply don't know what to think or believe about God.

I want to equip you for the massive task that stands before us. There's absolutely no doubt in my mind that if God can use me, He can use you too. How He works through our individual lives and how our stories unfold might be different, but in the end, they are equally as vital. As a generation, we have to awaken; we have to make the critical choices that transform our story into an epic, world-impacting legacy.

Your story doesn't start in 10 years or even 5 years. It starts now, while you're still young. It's time to jump in head first.

1 GOD'S HABIT

Did you ever develop a habit you just couldn't shake? No matter how passionately you try, somehow you naturally gravitate towards doing things a certain way. Did you know God has habits? All throughout the Bible, trends in God's behavior jump off the pages. It's hard to miss, but many times people still don't pay attention to it. God's track record overwhelmingly demonstrates that He really enjoys picking young people to take on big assignments. He places a ton of trust in their potential, in who they can be and what they can do.

Consider this. God sent His only Son to minister on the earth for 3 years, to die, rise from the dead, and get the church started. Jesus knew He would have 3 years to find and train a handful of people to take over His mission when He left. He had 3 years to determine those who would carry out His life and legacy after His brief ministry would end. Who does He choose? 12 young people. In fact, most biblical scholars believe 11 of the 12 disciples were still teenagers when Jesus first called them. What does that mean? Jesus Christ actually placed the entire future of the

Church in the hands of a college-age leadership. Is God crazy? Obviously not!

God knows something about the profound capacity of a young person. That's why the Scriptures say, "Don't let anyone look down on you because you are young, but set an example for the believers in speech, in life, in love, in faith, and in purity" (1 Timothy 4:12 NIV). He placed within a young person the ability to inspire and even lead all of God's people in literally every aspect of life.

If you are reading this book as a young person, or if there is a young person in your life that you are mentoring, it is probable you have never thought about God's massive faith in them. Young people are often thought of as unknowledgeable, irresponsible, inexperienced, and incapable. These ideas are reiterated so often in our society, that young people begin to believe them about themselves. In the days of Jeremiah, it was the same way.

God told Jeremiah that He wanted him to be His front man, His voice to an entire nation of people. The first thing Jeremiah shouts is "I am too young!" God adamantly replies, "Do not say, 'I am too young, for you must go wherever I send you and say whatever I command you" (Jeremiah 1:7 NLT). Jeremiah grew up in a patriarchal society where the mature adults and elders carried all the responsibility and absorbed all the respect. The father was the definitive head of the household and carried all of the authority. His wife and children were expected to obey him just as his slaves. Adults were to be honored and respected by children, and children were expected not to voice their opinions on adult-related issues. Their ideas didn't matter. As a rule, it is the same way in our society. Instead of our culture blatantly verbalizing, "you are incapable of doing anything great," our culture simply doesn't expect anything out of young people. Everyone's impressed when they don't get in too much trouble, stay away from drugs, get into college and start working in a decent-paying field.

The long-term effects of these low expectations are obvious in our society. It's nothing for a 30 year-old to still be "exploring" his/her options. The majority of people have no sense of their destiny or calling. Many adults continue living with their parents well into their late twenties and early thirties simply because they are too comfortable. They have nothing to live up to. Moms and dads expect less and less and shell out whatever their "child" demands, creating a culture of irresponsibility and entitlement.

> *The majority of people have no sense of their destiny or calling.*

For this reason, no one even entertains the idea of young people speaking to nations or making historic change. So, like many would react today, Jeremiah was shocked and backed away. Then, God began to challenge his thinking. He screams "Jeremiah! Wake up! I have an assignment that must be accomplished and you're My pick!" God wants to give some mind-blowing assignments to this next generation of young people. That's why He's waking us up and challenging the way we see ourselves and the possibilities of a life with Him. He's attempting to strip away the years of cultural conditioning that limit our expectations and keep us from running after the big.

Maybe no one in your life expects anything great out of you. You're considered a questionable candidate. Congratulations. God loves to exhibit His power through the lives of people others least expect. That's why the Scriptures say, "Instead, God chose things the world considers foolish in order to shame those who think they are wise. And he chose things that are powerless to shame those who are powerful" (1 Corinthians 1:27 NLT). Our culture screams that you have to look a certain way, dress a certain way, and act a certain way to make people follow you. In this verse, God says He wants to shame the people who are thought to be powerful and wise because of their looks, money, and everything else our culture worships. Do others consider you foolish? Do you think of yourself as powerless? Look at what God's saying here. You're the type of person He'll most likely choose because God can show off through you.

This was certainly the case in Mother Teresa's life, an unlikely candidate to shake the world. She was 12 when she began to feel a destiny for missions stirring inside. At 18, she left Skopje, Macedonia and began to teach at St. Mary's High School in Calcutta. On her way to teach at the school in the mornings, her heart would break as she saw hundreds of children asleep on the streets, sentenced to a life of devastating poverty. Even in the classroom, she would find herself staring out the windows at the children who didn't have a chance at receiving an education. One day she couldn't bear it anymore. She rushed into the school administrator's office and cried, "My mission is not in here; it's out there!" That day, the dream she held onto since the young age of 12 was born. Today, millions of neglected, broken people in poverty-stricken lands have been helped as a direct result of the movement she sparked. Over one million missionaries have been released all over the world through that one life.

It's God's habit. He grabs young people's hearts while they're still young. He doesn't usually wait until they're in their 30's, 40's, or 50's to stir their heart. Samuel, when he was a young boy, heard the voice of God in a time when the "the word of the LORD was rare... there was no widespread revelation" (1 Samuel 3:1 NKJV). How about Hezekiah? He became king of the entire nation at age 25! The Scriptures say, he "trusted in the LORD, the God of Israel. There was no one like him among all the kings of Judah, either before or after his time. He remained faithful to the LORD in everything, and he carefully obeyed all the commands the LORD had given Moses" (2 Kings 18:5-6 NLT). This young man's faith exceeded all the kings before and after him!

Josiah reigned as king from ages 8 to 39. In his 20's, he brought massive reformation to the nation. He not only destroyed idolatry in Israel, through his leadership the entire nation of people served the Lord without compromise. The Scriptures say of this young leader, "Josiah removed all detestable idols from the entire land of Israel and required everyone to worship the LORD their God. And throughout the rest of his lifetime, they did not turn away from the LORD, the God of their ancestors" (2 Chronicles 34:33 NLT).

God wants to do the same things through this generation that He did in the Bible.

God wants to do the same things through this generation that He did in the Bible. Most likely, He will not make you a king, but His plans for you far exceed your ability comprehend them. Maybe you'll create a website that changes culture, start a small business that generates profit for building orphanages, or write music that inspires change in people's life. The options are endless. However, as I have traveled and had one-on-one conversations with teenagers and college students across the world, I've discovered one unwavering similarity. There's a great deal of difference between our plans and God's plans, our ideas about our future and God's, His faith in us and our own. That is why God wants to take your heart, hold it in His loving hands and show you things to come. He wants to flood your mind with images of your future and bombard your spirit with understanding of your true potential in Him.

You don't have to wait. You can know what His will is for you and be confident in it right now. You can be one of the few that uniquely carries an exact knowledge of your calling and destiny. In this next chapter, I am going to teach you how to position your heart to receive God's dream for your life. Here goes.

2 RECEIVE THE DREAM

Every big dream has a specific birthplace. For some, it's dramatic, and for others it's subtle, but anyone who has accomplished anything of significance can look back at a certain time and a certain place when the dream for something great came alive in their heart.

If you've been going to church longer than 10 seconds, you've probably heard the phrase "God has a plan for your life" over and over again. I know I did. I went to a private elementary school where we had to memorize a new scripture every week. If we memorized two scriptures, we got extra stickers. My parents were also pastors, so that meant if the church doors were open, I was there. Believe it or not, at the age of 12, I truly thought I had learned all there is to know. I knew the major Bible stories and characters, could quote entire passages of scripture by memory, and heard the phrase "God has a plan for your life" 7,000 times. What did that translate to in reality? Absolutely nothing.

When I was younger, I wanted what all my friends wanted - to have fun. I figured one day when I graduated college, I would know God's plan for my life and it would be great when I got older. I assumed I would go through the normal motions of teenage and young adult life, and then, God would reveal His plan to me.

But God scheduled a meeting with me far sooner than the year I graduated college. In fact, I was only 12. It was a mid-week service at my parents' church. They had invited Dennis Tinerino, an ex-professional body builder and former Mr. Universe, to speak that night. He told his stories about bodybuilding, competing against Arnold Schwarzenegger, and how God had changed his life. Although he was a good speaker, my attention to his message was sporadic. I thought it was going to be just another week and another service on a Wednesday evening.

At the close of his message, he said, "If anyone in this room believes God has a special plan for their life, I want you to come forward, I'd like to pray for you." I was sitting with some friends, so I turned to them and said, "I think I'm going to go up there." No one else joined me. I walked to the front without much expectation and waited. As soon as Dennis prayed for me, I can hardly express with words what took place. I became instantly aware of God. It was so real and so strong; it was incomparable to anything I had ever felt.

After a few minutes, I began to see a vision. I saw enormous crowds of people. I saw thousands of people from all different cultures and ethnicities. The images were bold and real. Even more incredible than what I was seeing, though, was what I was feeling inside. I somehow knew the people I was seeing didn't know Christ, and I could literally feel God's aching heart for those people who were separated from Him. It was as if I had a glimpse of the pain in His heart for the lost. The sense of His enormous passion for them caused me to cry for nearly an hour.

As those tears ran down my face, my heart was being softened for the people of the world. Everything I had ever known was challenged. Suddenly going to the movies, hanging out, and playing sports all seemed so insignificant compared to what I had just experienced. I knew that somehow my life would be a part of helping those people, that God wanted me to be a part of changing those thousands of lives. At age 12, I began to receive God's dream for my life.

Just days before Jesus ascended to heaven and left the earth, He told a group of His followers to wait in Jerusalem. He made a promise that when He left He would not leave them without help. Instead, He would send them this person called the Holy Spirit, and the Holy Spirit will be with them forever. A handful of people listened to what Jesus said, and they waited in a room for this promise Jesus made. One morning while they were praying, a loud wind blew through the room and

As those tears ran down my face, my heart was being softened for the people of the world.

they were instantly overcome with the presence of God. They had never felt anything like it. Acts 2 says the presence of God was so overwhelming, the onlookers thought these people were drunk! Peter stood up to make sense of it all and shouted,

"'These people are not drunk, as some of you are assuming. Nine o'clock in the morning is much too early for that. No, what you see was predicted long ago by the prophet Joel: 'In the last days,' God says, 'I will pour out my Spirit upon all people. Your sons and daughters will prophesy. Your young men will see visions, and your old men will dream dreams'" (Acts 2:15-17 NLT).

Peter tried to explain that God is doing something massive, and it's not a coincidence. This moment in history was prophesied hundreds of years ago and promised to us by Christ himself. The Holy Spirit is here, and now everything is going to be different! Amazingly, the very first group of people mentioned is not the old people. It's not the elders and grandpas and grandmas. It's not the "mature" crowd. He talks about the young people! He references the sons, the daughters, and the young people first. He says in the last days, the Holy Spirit is going to move so profoundly in the young people they are going to start having visions and prophesying (speaking on behalf of God).

I now realize that this is what happened in my life. My experience on that Wednesday night was an exact fulfillment of this promise God made about the last days. It was an ordinary service for me, and then the Holy Spirit himself showed up. His power and presence overwhelmed me, and He gave me a vision. This is precisely what He wants to do for the entire rising generation of Christians. Some say, "Dominic that's because you have a special call from God, He doesn't do that with everyone." I have to disagree. The Bible says He is going to pour out His Spirit upon all people.

It doesn't say only "some" sons and "some" daughters will prophesy. It doesn't say "special" young men will see visions. You are included in the group "all people." That means now is the time for you to position your heart because, honestly, the Holy Spirit is ready to overwhelm you with His presence and give you a life-altering experience. He's waiting to download dreams and visions into your heart.

A football team can have the most talented quarterback in the league, but if the receivers never get into position, the quarterback will never make completions, and the team won't score. God is able and anxious to pour out His Holy Spirit in your life. He has no problem or reservation doing it, but you have to position yourself correctly. How do you get into position to receive from the Holy Spirit? Take a bold step towards Him. If your heart is not pointed in His direction, you can't expect to receive a dream from Him. James 4:8 NLT says, "Come close to God, and God will come close to you. Wash your hands, you sinners; purify your hearts, for your loyalty is divided between God and the world." Take a real look in your heart, and ask God to forgive you where you've compromised. After you have turned from your sin, be confident in His forgiveness and come close to Him. As you come close to the Spirit of God, He promises to come close to you. He is passionate for you.

As you come close to the spirit of God, He promises to come close to you. He is passionate for you.

Ephesians 3:12 says, "In him and through faith in him, we may approach God with freedom and confidence" (NIV). This is the type of Scripture you sometimes have to repeat a few times while you start taking steps towards God. It's so easy to feel condemned and unworthy when you approach God. Don't let your failures and shortcomings create an imaginary wall between you and God. It's just an illusion. The Word says plainly you can come with confidence and freedom. Why? Because Christ's death on the cross flattened every obstacle between you and God.

Engaging the Holy Spirit can be as simple as connecting with a good friend. Obviously, you recognize He's God, so there's a reverence and respect aspect to your communication. At the same time though, you can still communicate with Him as you would a friend. You can have open and honest moments of sharing the secrets of your heart with Him. You can tell Him your struggles and ask for help. You can tell Him your most passionate desires. But just as you would a friend, take some moments to listen as well. Don't keep the communication one-sided by doing all the talking. Expect the Spirit of God to talk back to you, and you will hear Him.

If you are engaging the Holy Spirit, you will receive God's dream for you. It will become so real to you that you won't be able to shake it. You will carry it like a pregnant woman carries a baby.

3 CAREFUL WITH THE BABY

Every single time I walk into an enormous jet airplane, and the plane begins to taxi on the runway, I think about how that steel cylinder is about to spend the next several hours at more than 35,000 feet in the air. The take-off always seems much more eventful than the flight. Sure, there are some rough patches once you've hit cruising altitude, but most of the turbulence always seems to come in the beginning. Turbulence during airplane take-off is especially dangerous because there is less margin for recovery. It is in the take-off stage when the jet burns the highest percentage of jet fuel because the aircraft requires the most energy and effort to make the climb. Not only that, this is when many accidents and crashes occur.

I think the enemy fully knows once we hit altitude, once we hit our stride, it's a lot more difficult to stand in our way. So he spends most of his time, effort, and planning on sabotaging our "take-off." He knows if he can get us to "mess up" on the runway, before our life ever takes off, he can keep us taxiing forever. If the devil is able to discourage us just as we're getting started, there is a smaller chance that our dream will take flight. That is why there is such a ruthless, direct assault against young people.

While you're receiving and working towards God's dream for you, the enemy works double-time to discourage and distract. He works through friends, circumstances, and negative thoughts to get you to doubt what God put inside you and most importantly, to give up on it. Friends will sometimes disapprove and be very vocal about it. Situations and challenges may present themselves totally out of left field. You'll have to deal with stuff that you never even knew existed! Sometimes, the enemy whispers malicious questions and lies in your mind like "Do you really think you can do that? You're not ready. You're a fake." It's important you push through all the turbulence during take-off and recognize the nature of the resistance to keep you grounded.

We all know that when a man and woman are intimate, a woman can conceive and get pregnant. What most people don't know is that it's the same with the Spirit of God and us. When we are intimate with the Holy Spirit, when we have one of those face-to-face encounters (like we discussed in chapter 2), the Holy Spirit himself places His dreams on the inside of us; we literally carry His dreams like a pregnant woman would carry a baby.

Did you ever stand in line at a theme park and notice a caution sign right before you were about to ride a roller coaster? Ten times out of ten, the sign communicates special caution for those who are pregnant, warning them not to ride the ride because it could injure the baby. For those who are pregnant, it is their primary responsibility to protect the life inside of them, so that eventually they can deliver a healthy baby. Obviously, not all pregnancies reach that point of delivery, and unfortunately, not everyone carrying dreams sees them come to pass.

As a young person, you carry that same important responsibility. No one can do it for you. Only you can protect that dream the Holy Spirit has put in your heart. Luke 1 tells the famous story of the angel Gabriel coming to Mary and announcing that Mary, the young teenager, was going to become pregnant with the Savior of the world. The first thing Mary said was, "How can this be?" The angel responds, "The Holy Spirit's power will overshadow you." In other words, Mary you're going to become pregnant supernaturally. Even though you haven't been intimate with a man, God himself is going to make you pregnant. It doesn't matter that you're young, it doesn't matter that you're inexperienced, the Holy Spirit is going to overshadow all of your shortcomings.

> *Only you can protect that dream the Holy Spirit has put in your heart.*

After Mary received the news, the Scriptures say, "A few days later Mary hurried to the hill country of Judea, to the town where Zechariah lived. She entered the house and greeted Elizabeth" (Luke 1:39-40, NLT). Mary hurries to the house of Elizabeth after receiving the news she was carrying the Messiah. Why? Because Elizabeth was also carrying a baby supernaturally, even in her old age, God enabled her to conceive John the Baptist.

Mary knew that if she was going to successfully complete her assignment to bring the Messiah to earth, she had to be with someone else who was also carrying something special from Heaven. So many times, young people go on a mission trip or go to a church camp or retreat and God does something profound in their heart. He gives them a glimpse of their future destiny. Soon after, they run back to the same surroundings, the same friends, and the same life. It's not that you have to kick out all your friends who aren't Christians from your life, but it's so important they don't remain in your inner circle. You can't just share the secrets of your heart with anyone. Remember what happened to Joseph, the ultimate dreamer, in the Old Testament? God gave him a dream that he would be a great leader. Joseph told his dream to all of his jealous brothers, and they set out to kill him. The book of Proverbs teaches only a fool reveals his whole heart.

Instead, we have to learn from Mary and keep ourselves surrounded with other people who know they are pregnant with an assignment from Heaven. When pregnant Mary greeted pregnant Elizabeth, John the Baptist jumped inside of her because of the presence of Jesus in Mary. When you surround yourself with people who have dreams from God, you will be encouraged and inspired by the supernatural dreams inside of them. When I was in college, I asked God to give me a handful of friends who took their call seriously. I found them, and they were a massive encouragement. To this day, I even work with most of them. We get to hang out non-stop. We travel the world together and continue to push each other to do things for God that are way bigger than ourselves or our abilities.

Remember Samson, the gifted Old Testament leader? When the Spirit of God would empower him, he led Israel into victory through countless battles. He was pregnant with the destiny to lead Israel into her greatest days. Instead of closely guarding that special call, he began to visit with women from other cities and other faiths. Ultimately, he aborted the "baby" he was carrying because he refused to protect it.

Another crucial key in seeing the dreams inside of you come to pass is having patience and understanding that there is a "due season." Just like a woman must patiently wait all nine months to experience a healthy delivery, we have to wait for the timing of God. I remember calling home from college talking to my Dad, frustrated and confused. I said, "Dad, how will I go to the nations of the world? I don't know anyone in Africa, Latin America, or Asia!" My Dad said, "Dominic, be patient. If God put it inside of you, God will bring it to pass." He reminded me of the powerful Scripture in 1 Peter 5:6, "Therefore humble yourselves under the mighty hand of God, that He may exalt you in due time" (NKJV). Everyone has a "due time," a season, a moment of delivery. Be patient and expectant, and don't get discouraged in the waiting process.

Let me be clear. Patience does not mean inactivity. Many of us sit around and do absolutely nothing because we are "waiting on God's timing." One of my mentors, Bob Harrison, often talks about Sir Isaac Newton's laws of motion, which state "A body in motion stays in motion. A body at rest stays at rest." He says it's so important you put the dreams of God in motion. Newton's laws reveal if something starts moving, it will keep moving even if it hits an obstacle. However, if something is totally at rest, it will stay that way. When God places a dream inside of you, you must constantly be doing something to get you to your goal. You will probably never have a master plan. God typically doesn't give an "A-Z" checklist, but He will likely give us A, B, and C. As we take a few small steps, it's amazing how the next steps become clear.

The summer after high school graduation I took a job in construction. I was placed in a crew that built large outdoor decks on the backs of people's homes. I will spare you the details of my contribution in that construction crew. Needless to say, I am confident I actually cost that company more than I made them (I somehow managed to break every piece of valuable equipment I got my hands on). I guess Russo's tend to be better "talkers" than manual laborers. At any rate, since I was on the bottom of the totem pole, I was always tasked with driving supplies around town to the different job sites. On those long drives across town, God continually put it in my heart to listen to a certain teaching CD where Bob Harrison talked about the law of dominant images. Just as soon as I would finish listening to it, God would say, "Listen to it again." I probably heard it over 25 times that summer.

In that teaching, Bob explained that humans are "visual beings" and that your life will always move in the direction of the most dominant image in your heart. Then he retells the story of Abraham and how God told Abraham to look at the stars of the sky and sand of the seashore. Undoubtedly, Abraham took a long look at those Mediterranean beaches and up those starry skies on dark nights. Then, God said to Abraham, "That's what your descendents will be like." Amazed, Abraham realizes it's impossible to even count the grains of sand and the stars in the nighttime sky. God gave

Abraham a picture, an image of his future because he knew Abraham would need it for the journey that stood before him. If you know the story, you'll remember Abraham had to wait decades before his wife Sarah had even one child. In fact, both he and his wife were physically beyond the age of producing children. God knew in those moments of discouragement and questioning, Abraham would need a picture, an image to refresh his faith, so every single night when the sun set and the stars emerged, he was again reminded of God's promise.

Since God led me listen to the entire CD 25 or more times, and I could probably quote most of it by memory, I took it seriously! When I walked into my dorm room my freshman year at O.R.U., one of the first things I did was ask my roommate Ben if I could borrow his printer. I emailed pictures of massive crowds and stadiums to his laptop and began printing those pictures. I stuck them up on the wall next to my bed and every night before I went to sleep, I saw those images of the multitudes. Every time I was working on a paper or studying the Bible, I could look over my shoulder and see the massive crowds of faces. Whenever I felt like giving up, those pictures would speak to me and motivate me to press on.

Surround yourself with images of your dreams. It works. The law of dominant images states that your life will always move in the direction of the most dominant image in your heart. I really believe it. The Bible says that Jesus "for the joy that was set before him" endured the cross (see Hebrews 12:2). What helped Him push through the agony of the cross were the images of you and me in a loving relationship with Him. When God gives you His dream, surround yourself with images of that dream.

What God has put on the inside of you is so priceless and unique; you have to guard it with all your heart. I believe every single God-inspired dream in your heart will come to pass. Remember, pregnant people can't do what everyone else does. They live with a different value system and a different understanding. They know that small sacrifices today equal massive rewards tomorrow. You carry something special in your spirit.

What God has put on the inside of you is so priceless and unique, you have to guard it with all of your heart.

What thing in your life is negatively affecting the dream of God inside of you from coming to pass? What or whom have you allowed in your life that needs to shift out? Who else do you know who is pregnant with the dreams of God that you can keep as a regular influence in your life? What can you do to get your dream in motion today? What images do you need to surround yourself with?

4 SPECIAL USE

Let's face it. The vast majority of young people are content with being normal. Even the vast majority of Christian young people are not living huge lives and accomplishing big things. Why? Because it's easier to be normal. When you are "normal", you fit in with everyone else. There's no pressure, lower expectations, and an overall easier ride. There's no goal to reach, no standard to meet, and most of all, there's no chance of failure. The fear of failure is such a dominating issue that much of the time, people decide to not try at all.

It's precarious because there are so many teenagers who are passionate about seeing their school revolutionized. There are so many college age and 20's who want to start world-impacting ministries, who want to launch businesses that fuel God's work, who want to do something historic before they get older.

We know God wants us to accomplish these huge dreams He's put inside of us. What is keeping us from reaching them? Maybe something tangible is in your way—a physical disability, a lack of time, family support, or money.

Maybe it's your own fear of failure or the people you are surrounding yourself with, like we talked about in Chapter 3. Usually, though, it is ourselves who are in the way of walking in greatness.

I'll never forget one January praying for the upcoming New Year. I was asking God to bless the year and to bring massive growth in my life. As I was rattling off all the things I wanted God to do through my life, He stopped me and took me to a certain part of Scripture that was written to the young leader Timothy. Here it is:

> In a wealthy home some utensils are made of gold and silver, and some are made of wood and clay. The expensive utensils are used for special occasions, and the cheap ones are for everyday use. If you keep yourself pure, you will be a special utensil for honorable use. Your life will be clean, and you will be ready for the Master to use you for every good work. Run from anything that stimulates youthful lusts. Instead, pursue righteous living, faithfulness, love, and peace. 2 Timothy 2:20-22 NLT

Through this passage, God explained that if I wanted Him to open up doors and give me the things I was asking for, I was going to have to lead a life that few are willing to lead. He said, "Dominic, what was OK for you last year is not OK for you this year. It's time to raise the bar."

This scripture makes it so clear: Many people get common, "everyday" level assignments, but some people receive extraordinary assignments. The determining factor in God's delegations hinge on the tiny but mighty word "if."

God said, "If you keep yourself pure, you will be a special utensil for honorable use!" From that point on, I could never forget that purity is the prerequisite for accomplishing massive things with God.

Think about it. Would you want to eat out of a dirty bowl or use a fork that was crusted over with old, dried food, even if it was made out of the finest china or silver? Of course not. At least, not until they were thoroughly washed. It's the same with God. It's hard for Him to use us in the special way He intends until we have purified our lives. We have to embrace the value in staying consistently clean. When we allow junk and sin to build up inside our hearts, we are far less useful in God's hands.

God is scanning our generation, and there are a handful of us who are catching His eye. Those who have made bold, resolved commitments to live pure in every aspect of their lives attract God's attention. Upon this small group, God looks down and says, "special use."

God is scanning our generation, and there are a handful of us who are catching His eye.

Mark this down. The enemy is working intentionally and passionately to distract and pollute our hearts. He knows that purity is so critical to the fulfillment of our destiny. He knows that it is the number one criterion God has established. That's why it is important that we recognize and aggressively stand against his intentions. Check out this Scripture:

You will be accepted if you do what is right. But if you refuse to do what is right, then watch out! Sin is crouching at the door, eager to control you. But you must subdue it and be its master. Genesis 4:7 NLT

What fierce language! Sin is waiting and constantly working to control us; we have to make the decision to "subdue" it and be its master or else it will prevail. One of the fruits of the Holy Spirit's presence in our lives is self-control. This is a helpful quality in staying away from all types of sin. The problem is that we live in a body with temptations constantly hitting us. Flip on the TV and there's temptation. Open your laptop and there's temptation. Take a casual stroll in the mall and Victoria is showing you all her secrets. It's impossible to escape the temptations. So, how do we do it? Jesus tells us:

Blessed are those who hunger and thirst for righteousness, for they will be filled. Matthew 5:6 NIV

We must crave purity more than the air we breathe. Jesus said to hunger and thirst for it. He first preached this sermon to a group of folks in the first century. When they needed to get somewhere, they weren't dropping the top on the convertible and heading out. They were walking! They would walk for hours under the Middle Eastern sun, without an opportunity to 'think outside the bun' when they had a craving for a hummus filled chalupa. These guys didn't have water fountains to visit or 24 packs of Dasani when their throats grew parched. They had to wait until they got to a well or to their final destinations. Within this context,

Jesus said blessed are those who hunger and thirst. You gotta want it, and you gotta want it bad.

Hebrews 12:14 tells us to, "pursue holiness." Purity and holiness before God will never just happen by accident. It comes to those who pursue it. I learned what it means to pursue a few years back when I started dating my wife Lindsay. Lindsay grew up in Kansas, and she always told herself the last thing she would do is travel often and leave home. I knew the call of God on my life included a boat load of travel, so I had my work cut out for me. I had to show her how much I valued her and desired her to live life with me. When it finally came time to say "I love you" for the first time, I made sure it was unforgettable. I took her to New York City for the day and whisked her around to every cool spot I could find. Every second was planned. Then, at the end of the night, I convinced the manager of a big hotel to give me exclusive use of his restaurant on the top floor of the property. At midnight, under the stars and with the city lights glowing through the glass walls, I played their grand piano and sang, "I Can't Help Falling in Love with You." When it came time to propose, I surprised her with a trip to London and dropped to my knee in front of Buckingham Palace. I asked her to be my "princess for life." She said yes, and we haven't stopped traveling the world since that time. I know what it means to pursue something or someone. It takes focus, energy and a whole lot of work. That's the kind of attention living with purity and holiness requires. I will promise you this: Purity always enters the heart of those that fervently seek it.

Every single person has the same temptations. "The temptations in your life are no different from what others experience. And God is faithful. He will not allow the temptation to be more than you can stand. When you are tempted, he will show you a way out so that you can endure" (1 Corinthians 10:13 NLT).

The people who overcome temptations are those who humble themselves and cry out for purity. Now more than ever, I have to get on my knees and ask God for grace to remain pure. Temptations never go away. As young people, we need to get in the habit of dominating them. Give God free reign in your life. Tell Him your innermost thoughts and struggles, even though He already knows what they are. Your honesty and authenticity before God moves His heart.

> *The people who overcome temptations are those who humble themselves and cry out for purity.*

Are you struggling with your purity? Are you giving in to temptation? If so, talk to your pastor or a spiritual leader and begin to passionately ask God for grace to overcome them. Your destiny is so much more valuable than a temporary "thrill." Your calling is so much more precious than the destructive path of sin.

Maybe there are no major areas of concern, but there are small areas in your life that you know need to change. Paul wrote, "Don't you realize that this sin is like a little yeast that spreads through the whole batch of dough?" (1 Corinthians 5:6 NLT). Song of Solomon says it is the "little foxes that spoil the vine." Don't justify them away in your head. Overcome them.

Throughout my teen years, my favorite worship song was

called "No Compromise." Jim Stern wrote these powerful lyrics:

"Lord, look into my heart and look into my life and tell me what You see. I choose to walk the straight and narrow path and not the way that's easy. A double-minded man cannot stand against the storms of evil. So, make my life a sacrifice at keeping your commands. This is my prayer; this is my longing, no compromise."

Lord, our prayer is that we would have hearts that are blameless, holy and pure. We want to be able to be called upon for "special, honorable use." Make our lives free from compromise. Convict us when we depart from Your truth, and may Your kindness forever lead us to a place of repentance.

5 LIKE A FIRE

Have you ever told someone about Jesus? Most people haven't. Most people have never opened their mouth and shared their faith. Some say, "It's just not my personality type to be outspoken." Others admit they are just plain fearful. To make matters worse, the culture in the U.S. increasingly shuns all expressions of evangelism. Society teaches us that religion should be a "personal" thing and that sharing your faith is "forcing your beliefs" on someone else. We are taught to be politically correct and not offend others with our ideas. It seems like the only law most people know about is the separation between church and state. They're working hard to keep us quiet: in school, at work, and even with friends.

In spite of this, did you know there are actually people rising up from all four corners of the planet who are marked with wild boldness? The most unassuming people, especially young people, are completely fearless. Proverbs 28:1 explains, "…the righteous are as bold as a lion." When I was fifteen, I spent a month in Ghana, West Africa and returned for two weeks when I was 17. I stared at a several hundred pound albino lion from only 7 feet away; we were eyeball to eyeball. Let me tell you there is nothing remotely timid about lions. They never avoid a challenge, and they certainly never cower in fear. This Scripture compares those ferocious beasts to us when our hearts connect with God. God offers us the raw courage to face anyone at anytime regardless of the resistance. Just this past summer, I heard about a 14 year-old girl named Kiara in Lima, Peru. Just two weeks after she got saved, she scrounged up the money to rent a small building near her neighborhood to hold a church service. She invited every single one of her friends, family and neighbors to come out and hear about Jesus. In that one night, and because of her courageous faith, 35 of them gave their lives to Christ.

Jesus was fearless, and His fearlessness was contagious. He confronted all His opposition with ease because He knew who He was and who was backing Him up. He did not allow the opinions and threats of man to drag him away from His assignments. This way of life rubbed off on some of the disciples. Acts 4:13 says, "Now when they saw the boldness of Peter and John, and perceived that they were uneducated and untrained men, they marveled. And they realized that they had been with Jesus" (NKJV). Peter and John were not Harvard grads, or even college grads for that matter. They were fishermen. They were blue collar. Yet their time with Jesus so transformed their entire persona, it absolutely shocked everyone. Whether you know it or not, your time with Jesus is changing you. You too are about to shock everyone around you. No one will be able to understand what changed or how you went from a timid follower to a voice that resonates with authority from heaven. They'll recognize it has to be Jesus.

One of the greatest promises in the entire Bible is found in Acts 2:17. It reads, "'In the last days, 'God says', I will pour out my Spirit upon all people. Your sons and daughters will prophesy…NLT.'" This is wild! God promises to pour out his Spirit on all, and again, the first group He addresses is the young people! Amazingly, it does not say your pastors and ministers will prophesy. It says the sons and daughters will. It doesn't say they might prophesy; it says they will prophesy.

The obvious question becomes "What does it mean to prophesy?" Prophecy is not a 50-year old man in a nice suit speaking about the future using large, 18th century vernacular, such as "And God sayeth unto thee" or "Thus sayeth the Lord…". Although sometimes a message from God does come in that packaging, the word "prophecy" simply means "to speak on behalf of God" or "to communicate God's heart." Prophecy is not some ultra-mystical, super-spiritual phenomena. It doesn't necessarily mean you can tell the future; it doesn't make you a Christian fortune teller. Sometimes, the word "prophecy" has a negative stigma in the church. But true prophecy is when God reaches down from heaven, overcomes your heart with His passion, and in-turn you speak on His behalf to your generation.

This scripture says the young people will prophesy. That means that you are going to begin speaking the heart of God. God is going to place a thought, a string of ideas, a feeling so strongly within you that you will have to speak it, regardless of your age. Maybe you have never considered yourself a "speaker" or a "prophet." You don't have to be any of those things. You just have to go after it a little bit. Let the Holy Spirit get a good grip on your heart, and ask

God for it! There may be just one person in your life who so desperately needs a word from God they are on the verge of calling it quits. Maybe there's a group of your friends who need to be inspired by your faith-filled encouragement. Or maybe some of the older people in your life need to be refreshed through your revelation. All of these things are considered prophesy when partnered with the inspired help of the Holy Spirit. The Bible says, "…eagerly desire spiritual gifts, especially the gift of prophecy" (1 Corinthians 14:1 NIV). Ask God again and again to fill with you with His spirit and to enable you to prophesy in a greater way. God likes when we ask Him to transform us into a bold voice for Him.

If you like what I'm saying, but you're still pushing back on this whole idea of speaking for God, you're not alone. More than snakes, poisonous spiders, heights, and even death itself, the sweeping majority of the human race fears being in the spotlight. Just the thought of being in front of people produces legitimate anxiety. Even young people avoid speaking in front of their friends, let alone people two and three times their age. One of my favorite stories in the Bible offers a sneak peak of God dropping the "bomb" on a young man about his call to speak for him. Here's what happened.

> The LORD gave me this message: "I knew you before I formed you in your mother's womb. Before you were born I set you apart and appointed you as my prophet to the nations." "O Sovereign LORD," I said, "I can't speak for you! I'm too young!" The LORD replied, "Don't say, 'I'm too young,' for you must go wherever I send you and say whatever I tell you. And don't be afraid of the people,

for I will be with you and will protect you. I, the
LORD, have spoken!"

Jeremiah 1:4-8 NLT

God told Jeremiah that He knew him before he was
born and called him to be His voice. Take a close look at
what Jeremiah said, "I can't speak for you because I'm too
young!" Jeremiah basically said, God
we both know this assignment lies far
outside of my capability and, most
importantly it assumes far too much.
No one is going to listen to what I have
to say". God said, "Do not say you are
too young. You must go wherever I
send you and say whatever I tell you"
(Jeremiah 1:7/my paraphrase). He
finishes his reply by shouting "I, the
LORD, have spoken!" In other words,
"I spoke the entirety of the universe into existence and it
now is." See, we can't even attempt to wrestle with our
destiny; it's already in motion just by virtue of the fact that
God said it is!

> *See, we can't
> even attempt to
> wrestle with our
> destiny; it's al-
> ready in motion
> just by virtue of
> the fact that God
> said it was!.*

Here's what's unreal. Most biblical scholars now label
this same, fear-stricken Jeremiah as "the weeping prophet."
At some point between God calling Jeremiah and Jeremiah's
launch, God began to break Jeremiah's heart for his nation
until he would weep for the sin of his generation.

Has that ever happened to you? Have you ever walked
through the halls of your middle school, high school or college
and just wanted to cry because of the darkness and lack of

hope? Have you ever heard the conversations at work the Monday after one of their "crazy" weekends? Has the sin of our generation begun to break your heart? If the answer is yes, you are on your way to becoming a mouthpiece for God. That's what happened inside of Jeremiah. As his heart began to break, God placed a message in his heart. He placed a heavy word in his mouth.

Eventually, the once fearful Jeremiah would shout, "... His word is in my heart like a fire, a fire shut up in my bones. I am weary of holding it in; indeed, I cannot" (Jeremiah 20:9 NIV). The very same Jeremiah who cried, "I am too young" is now shouting "If I don't speak I am going to explode!" Suddenly, a message burned in his soul that he had to let escape.

Your tears and your heartbreak for the compromises in your generation will become your message. As God takes your heart in his hand and lets you feel His emotions, everything about you will begin to change. The fact that eating disorders are growing more and more pervasive might begin to bother you. The fact that teen and young adult suicide is at an all time high may start to provoke you. The reality that millions of orphaned children are living without a home might shake you up. Whatever is it that breaks your heart will become your message. The tears you shed will actually build your platform; it will create your unique sound in our generation.

The very same things God promised Jeremiah He promises you today. God's been saying some remarkable things about your destiny. Before you attempt to excuse away your candidacy, remember God never gives His people an assignment without a promise. You were chosen by God, He will be with you, and you must never fear. Staggeringly, God hand picked you and crafted your calling in life before you were even conceived. Your existence on this planet was never a surprise for God. It transcends the decision of your mother and father. You carry a calling on your life that began in the very heart and mind of God. Psalm 139:16 NIV says, "...your eyes saw my unformed body. All the days ordained for me were written in Your book before one of them came to be." Jeremiah 29:11 NIV says, "I know the plans I have for you, declares the LORD, "Plans to prosper you and not to harm you, plans to give you hope and a future." Doesn't it feel good to know that God has a plan? He knows what's happening in your life, He knows what is going to happen, and it's going to be good, (see 2 Thessalonians 1:11)

Most of the people around us are fearful, filled with anxiety and uncertainty. This is why we must carry hope to our world.

One of my mentors called me last week and said, "Dominic, today's the worst day of the rest of our lives and today was pretty darn good." I like that. Proverbs communicates that the path of the righteous gets brighter and brighter like the dawning of a new day. For us Christians, life just gets better. We are infused with hope for our future. Most of the people around us are fearful, filled with anxiety and uncertainty. This is why we must carry hope to our world.

I made a decision a couple years ago that everyday I want to be in the conversations of God. Every single day I want my name to be discussed in heaven. Jesus said, "If you acknowledge me before men, I will acknowledge you before my father in heaven!" (Matthew 10:21.) That means when I raise my voice and bring the name of Jesus to my generation, Jesus raises His voice and talks about me to God! Think about it. Jesus said when one sinner repents, all of heaven rejoices! That means heaven knows what's happening here on earth. The angels know when we are talking about Jesus and they especially know when people receive His salvation because they party hard. I sometimes think about how cool it would be if one day the angels and God alike said, "Look at that Dominic – he's wild! He just won't shut up about us. He's telling the whole world about us!" Wouldn't it be sweet if Jesus started acknowledging your name before the Father? Let His message burn in you like a fire and release it every single day.

6 ONLY ASK

Growing up in an Italian family entails certain unwavering traditions. Memorial Day carried a unique tradition in the Russo family. Each one was spent at the pool in Grandpa Russo's backyard. I have 16 cousins – 8 guys and 8 girls, and every year the scene looked identical. All 8 of the girl cousins would lay out in the sun while all 8 of the guy cousins engaged in the water game of champions. The game was simple, but it entertained us for hours at a time. A raft was thrown in the deep end of the pool, and one person would battle to stay on top. That is, until they were violently overthrown by someone in the water.

I'll never forget one Memorial Day in particular because for the first time, I had officially graduated from my "floaties." That's right. The water wings were gone once and for all, and I was as egotistical as a six-year-old could be. I jumped into the deep-end before any other of my cousins, climbed on the raft, and called for my cousins to come and start the "war." Well, within eight seconds, I was ripped off the top by one of my stronger, faster cousins. My tiny, brown body plunged underneath the water and I quickly began to swim back up to the surface. As I awkwardly struggled to get above the water, my head hit the bottom of the raft. I swam to the left, struggled to get to the surface but couldn't. I swam to the right – same result. Remember, this was my first time in the deep end of the pool without any flotation device. I was terrified.

The sensation of panic that fills your mind when you're under water and can't breathe totally overcame me. Finally, after a few more frantic attempts, I pushed my head above the surface of the water, took a deep breath, and screamed at the top of my lungs "Heeeeelp!" That was the first thing that came out of my mouth!

Meanwhile, my dad was eating dinner with my aunts and uncles. He was wearing the usual 'deigo' attire - dress pants, a silk-short sleeved shirt, sandals, and of course, a gold chain nestled comfortably in his chest hair (sorry, Dad). At the very second he heard my cry for help, he literally jumped from the dinner table, dove totally clothed into the deep end, put his arm around me, and swam me into the shallow end. Without even a second's hesitation, he responded at the sound of my cry.

That day I learned about my father's wholehearted commitment to me. It wasn't until several years later that I learned about the wholehearted commitment of my Heavenly Father. I was a 15 year-old freshman in high school. Walking through the halls, I was constantly plagued with the thought – *do the people around me have a relationship with God?* It seemed like everywhere I turned, I heard a conversation about getting smashed in the upcoming weekend, sleeping around, or smoking weed.

God began to stir my freshman heart. My youth pastor constantly challenged us to reach out to friends and people at school who might not know Christ. So, I began to ask God something BIG. I began to pray daily for God to save my entire high school. I held onto a vision that every single student in my high school would lift their hands to Jesus and pray the prayer of salvation. Every time I shut my eyes, I could just picture those hands lifting in the air. Many nights I would close the door to my bedroom, play some worship music, and just begin to pray with all my heart. On several occasions, I cried out to God with all of my strength for him to shake my high school and save every person who was confused, trapped in sin, and separated from Him.

My freshman year went by and nothing dramatic seemed to transpire. Then my sophomore and junior years passed and still nothing major happened. There were times throughout those first three years when people in my class prayed the prayer of salvation or went to church with me. Still my heart was dissatisfied. I wanted with all my heart to see every hand in my entire school lifted up to Jesus Christ. I continued to pray and cry out to God.

One day Jesus told a story about prayer and how to get your prayers answered.

"There was a judge in a certain city," he said, "who neither feared God nor cared about people. A widow of that city came to him repeatedly, saying, 'Give me justice in this dispute with my enemy.' The judge ignored her for a while, but finally he said to himself, 'I don't fear God or care about people, but this woman is driving me crazy. I'm going to see that she gets justice, because she is wearing me out with her constant requests!'"

Then the Lord said, "Learn a lesson from this unjust judge. Even he rendered a just decision in the end. So don't you think God will surely give justice to his chosen people who cry out to him day and night? Will he keep putting them off? I tell you, he will grant justice to them quickly! But when the Son of Man returns, how many will he find on the earth who have faith?"

Luke 18:2-8 NLT

Look at the picture Jesus is painting. There's an old, helpless widow and there's an authoritative, ruling judge. The judge has money and power. The widow lacks any social influence. The widow has a problem that requires the help of the court, so she petitions this judge relentlessly. The judge blows her off at first, but finally grants justice to the lady on account of her tireless persistence. Then Jesus looks square in the eyes of all the hearers and essentially says, "If a wicked judge will answer a persistent widow – how much more will your Heavenly Father respond to His own kids!" He ends it by saying God will respond "quickly."

Just like my dad responded immediately to the sound of my cry, so God responds to the persistent cry of his sons and daughters. I believe all three years God was hearing my cry in high school. Finally, my senior year came. I approached the principal of our entire high school and asked him a bold request – to authorize me to hold a mandatory school-wide assembly during school hours. He responded with words that I'll never forget – "That is not a precedent I wish to establish." Refusing to quit, I sold the idea to the president of the student body. She was the apple of the principal's eye. Once she owned the vision and presented it to the principal, he looked at us and said, "OK!" Finally, all 1,200 students packed into the gymnasium! I invited a special group called "The Power Team" to the assembly. They broke bricks and performed feats of strength to capture everyone's attention. At the close of the event, James Henderson, the strongest man in the world, said "If you are ready to accept the forgiveness of Jesus Christ and begin a personal relationship with God, lift your hands now!" I began to cry as ALL 1,200 of the students shot their hands in the air and prayed a salvation prayer.

I learned that day that God is eager to answer, but He's waiting for His sons and daughters to ask. Many times, young people pray and when nothing happens, they stop. Jesus said that we have to be like that persistent widow. We have to cry out! We have to be resilient. We have to come passionately into the presence of God and ask and keep on asking! I've often wondered what is so special to God about crying out. Why can't we just whisper to Him every time we pray? Certainly, God does not have a hearing problem. Then, it dawned on me. Jesus ended His story about the widow by saying "but when the Son of man comes will he really find faith on the earth?" Crying out is an act of faith. No one in their right mind would persistently cry out at the top of their lungs to a God they didn't wholeheartedly believe was listening! Our resilience moves the heart of God.

Psalms 2:8 NLT states, "Only ask and I will give you the nations as your inheritance." God wants to give the rising generation the salvation of entire nations; He's just waiting for them to ask. I firmly believe you can ask God for 1 person to be saved through your life, and He will give you that 1 life. I also firmly believe you can ask God for 10 people, even 100 or 1,000 people. But He's waiting on us to ask! Jeremiah 33:3 says, "Call to Me, and I will answer you, and show you great and mighty things, which you do not know" (NKJV). We have to call! We have to cry out! So few in our generation are doing it. He's ready to show us great and mighty things.

> *God wants to give the rising generation the salvation of entire nations; He's just waiting for them to ask.*

A few months back I was in the home of one my mentors, Dr. T. L. Osborn. Through Dr. Osborn's ministry, thousands and even millions came to Christ in the 1900's. The man carries so much wisdom. At one point in our conversation, he looked intently at me and said, "I believe God is ready and waiting for us. I love your plans to reach nations. Dominic, God is clapping!" Wow. What an image of God we don't typically have. Now when I pray, I imagine God sitting at the edge of His throne, passionate and ready to answer our prayers, especially for the salvation of nations.

This is your moment to learn how to move heaven with your prayers. You need to stand before God, bring the dreams and visions of your heart before Him, and cry out. Cry out with every fiber of your being. The Bible says, "The righteous cry out and the LORD hears them" (Psalm 34:17 NIV) Everything you have ever needed, presently need, or will ever need is trapped in heaven. When you cry out, it brings all of heaven directly into your world. Avoid the "waiting on God" mindset. Jesus commanded us to pray that God's will and kingdom would come to this earth.

Here's the big question: Have you asked?

7 WHEN IT'S NOT FUN, DON'T RUN

Jesus didn't always win the popularity contest. Let's be honest. He ticked people off so badly they publicly beat and killed Him. Sure, He had his moments when the masses sang His praise and shouted His name with pride. He had moments when 25,000 people followed Him like ants, when His miracles brought wine to a wedding reception and food to thousands of families, when He raised a dear friend from the dead. The Bible says His fame exploded after that one. At the end of the day, though, he was a controversial man. Either you loved Him or you hated His very existence.

When young people get saved and give their lives over to Christ, often times they are shocked when tough things start taking place. I know I was. I'll never forget the moment I walked into my World Literature class during my sophomore year of high school. As I passed through the doorway, suddenly one of the most popular girls in school started screaming, "Here comes Jesus riiiiding on his donkey. Wave the palm branches. Waaaave the palm branches. He's here to save us all!" Shocked and embarrassed, I walked to my desk, and the bell rang to start class. That 45-minute class seemed like an eternity. As soon as class ended, I jumped up to leave as quickly as possible, and the same girl that mocked me as I was entering the class ran up ahead of me and turned around. She corned me in front of everyone and with full 'Mean Girls' type enthusiasm shouted, "Dominic Russo!"

"Ya?" I muttered.

"I don't know what you think you're trying to do at this school," she continued. "This whole thing of you trying to save everyone is stupid, and I want you to know something. I will never come to your church." (I had invited her to my youth group at church a few times).

"That's totally fine," I replied, and she stormed away in frustration.

The entire rest of the day, I felt like an utter and complete failure because I was passionately trying to get the people in my school to move towards God, not away from God. I left school that day totally discouraged, wondering if that's how everyone in my class felt about me, but only that girl was honest enough to speak up. It was a Wednesday, so that night I went to my church's youth service. Mid way through, I left to use the restroom. As I walked across the lower level of the church, I looked over my shoulder and saw two people walk through the double doors. To my total shock, it was the same girl from my World Literature class, and she brought a friend. I walked right up to them and said, "It's so great to see..."

She immediately cut me off and said, "We were just in the area and decided to stop by." A year later she "stopped by" the church again and walked to the front at the end of a service to give her life to Christ.

All obedience comes with a cost. I was obeying what Jesus commands us to do – I was telling people about Him! Yet, the more I obeyed, the more resistance and opposition I attracted from the people around me. One day, I started thinking about all the "heroes" of the Bible and their life stories. I realized that every single one of them had a ton of moments that were everything but "fun." Over and over again, when they obeyed God, things seemed to get far worse before they got better.

I thought of Noah. Here's a guy who gets an order from Heaven to build a boat, a boat large enough to contain a pair of every living creature. As if that wasn't extreme enough, God tells him to build the boat because an enormous flood was about to hit. Now, if he lived near the Caribbean or around the Pacific Rim, that might not be too bad of a task, considering all the hurricanes and tsunamis. But, it had never rained. Not even once. Still, Noah obeyed God, and in return, he was awarded decades of mockery and ridicule. He was more than likely the butt of every joke and the headline of every paper. His kids probably never heard the end of it. All because he did what God told him to do!

Then, I remembered Daniel, a man of unshakeable faith. He quickly progressed in the national government and was granted a high-ranking administration role under King Darius. Some of the other administrators, fueled by jealousy towards Daniel, pressured the king to officially decree that for 30 days, no man was to worship or pray to any god or person except him. If anyone broke this law, they would be cast into a den of ferocious lions. Daniel refused to compromise his prayer life and continued to go upstairs, open his window, and pray to the one true God three times per day. In return for his allegiance to God, he was hurled into a den of hungry lions. Obedience equaled lions den.

What about Shadrach, Meshach and Abednego? These were young guys training under a powerful empire when the king formulated a wicked law. King Nebuchadnezzar commanded the entirety of the nation to bow down and worship their false gods. If anyone transgressed this command, they were promised a spot in a blazing furnace of fire. They had a predicament to contemplate. Obey God and burn, or disobey God and be celebrated. These boys decided obedience to God surpassed the promise of security, so they refused to bow. In return, they were bound hand and foot then shoved into the furnace. Obedience meant torturous flames.

What about the New Testament people like Paul? Same thing. Jesus commissioned him to preach, so he preached wholeheartedly. Here's a detailed picture of what Paul explains obedience earned him.

"I have worked harder, been put in prison more often, been whipped times without number, and faced death again and again. Five different times the Jewish leaders gave me thirty-nine lashes. Three times I was beaten with rods. Once I was stoned. Three times I was shipwrecked. Once I spent a whole night and a day adrift at sea. I have traveled on many long journeys. I have faced danger from rivers and from robbers. I have faced danger from my own people, the Jews, as well as from the Gentiles. I have faced danger in the cities, in the deserts, and on the seas. And I have faced danger from men who claim to be believers but are not. I have worked hard and long, enduring many sleepless nights. I have been hungry and thirsty and have often gone without food. I have shivered in the cold, without enough clothing to keep me warm."

2 Corinthians 11:23b-27 NLT

Paul does what is right, and a lot of wrong things happen. In fact, in addition to all these troubles, he spends a considerable amount of time in prison.

Finally, I considered the ultimate example, Jesus Christ himself. The Bible explains that Christ lived a perfect, sinless life. Every day He lived, He was in total connection to the perfect plan of God. He never deviated, never stumbled. Everything the Father told Him to say, He said, and everything the Father told Him to do, He did. He loved people, He operated in compassion, He blessed the human race, and He obeyed God flawlessly. What did His perfect life of obedience produce? The cross.

Have you recently made a decision to step things up and follow God at a higher level? Have you determined in your heart to obey Him and to uncompromisingly follow Him to wherever He tells you to go and do whatever He tells you to do? If the answer is yes, then you have probably realized it's not always fun. However, listen carefully. When it's not fun, don't run! God is working in your place of challenge. One hundred percent of the time, there's something extraordinary in motion.

I've noticed every challenge in my life, including the one in my sophomore World Literature class, eventually dissolves and transforms into something miraculous. I now see how God enjoys operating. Because although Noah was the laughing stock of the city, he saved his entire family when the rest of the world was destroyed. When Daniel was trapped in the den of lions, not a single lion touched him, and it totally floored the king and kingdom. Shadrach, Meshach and Abednego got tossed into the fiery furnace, yet not a single flame was capable of singeing their skin or clothes. When Paul was thrown in prison, he transcribed the most profound books of the Bible. Even though Jesus was publicly humiliated and crucified, we love and worship Him today because He came alive after that death. I began to see that the lions weren't strong enough, the furnace was not hot enough, Paul's prison was not secure enough, and Christ's grave was not large enough to contain the masterful plan and deliverance of God.

God will use your troubles, your story and the opposition you face for being a true Christ-follower to wildly display His wisdom.

When it's not fun, don't run! God is working everything out for your good. (See Romans 8:28.) God will use your troubles, your story and the opposition you face for being a true Christ-follower to wildly display His wisdom. See through your trials and recognize that God will absolutely never leave you hanging. He promises, "I will never leave you nor forsake you" ,Hebrews 13:5 NKJV).

Here's what needs to happen. You have to prepare yourself, so than when tough times come you won't bail out. "So then, since Christ suffered... you must arm yourselves with the same attitude he had, and be ready to suffer, too' 1 Peter 4:1 NLT. You need to arm your mind and your heart. When soldiers go to battle, they aren't shocked when bombs are bursting and bullets are flying by because they've been prepared for it. I am warning you now that oppositions and hardships inevitably come when you obey God. Jesus said, ""If the world hates you, remember that it hated me first. 19 The world would love you as one of its own if you belonged to it, but you are no longer part of the world. I chose you to come out of the world, so it hates you" John 15:18-19 NLT. Jesus explains that because you are different, because you follow Him, people will at some point hate you.

Look at what Peter said:

Dear friends, don't be surprised at the fiery trials you are going through, as if something strange were happening to you. Instead, be very glad—for these trials make you partners with Christ in his suffering, so that you will have the wonderful joy of seeing his glory when it is revealed to all the world. So be happy when you are insulted for being a Christian, for then the glorious Spirit of God rests upon you."

1 Peter 4:12-14 NLT

Instead of getting sad, instead of running, start getting massively excited because God's own Spirit is going to literally rest upon you.

When it's not fun, don't you dare run.

8 ESCAPE TO ELEVATE

One of my closest childhood friends, Gabe, is one of the coolest and most well-liked guys I know. However, after high school, he underwent a bit of a rough patch in his spiritual life. You can say he 'bent the law' a time or two. I am in no way condoning what he did, in fact, I am advising you not to try this at home. But here's what happened.

Throughout high school, Gabe was the lead singer of a band and eventually grew to love live shows and concerts. Every time a major tour came to our region, he tried to go. One year his favorite band's concert completely sold out before he could buy tickets, and he was livid. All he could do was envision those 20,000 fans screaming, having the time of their lives while he sat at home. Frustrated, his creative mind started devising a plan. He jumped onto Ebay and located an all-access pass to one of the band's previous concert tours that someone had posted online to sell as a souvenir. He copied an image of the pass, dragged it into Photoshop and modified the dates to reflect the present year's concert tour. After altering the image, he got it professionally cut and laminated. Ten minutes later, he drove to the Palace of Auburn Hills, one of Michigan's largest venues, and flashed the backstage pass to the parking attendants. Instead of making him pay, they quickly said, "Right this way." After coasting through the parking lot, he hurried to the main entrance and, again, flashed his fake pass. Without hesitation, security escorted him straight to the backside of the stage where he enjoyed the best seat in the house throughout the entire concert. Instantly, they granted him all-access because that little card authorized him to go wherever he pleased. Not long after, he may or may not have pulled the same scam for another huge event. Thankfully, my good friend Gabe is now a changed man and actually purchases tickets when he wants to see a show.

Using that example, you have to admit it would be pretty sweet if you could have an all-access pass to hang out with one of your favorite celebs or bands anytime you wanted. Ironically, the Bible also talks about a sort of 'all-access' pass that Christ's sacrificial death on the cross provided for us.

The entire Bible details the dramatic story of how it all went down. The Scriptures explain that Adam and Eve used to walk and talk with God, but sin disqualified them from that close friendship. Their disobedience produced a giant division between God and his children. Because God so fervently desired to connect with His people, He began entering back into our world in different forms throughout history. The Bible vividly shows how God kept moving closer and closer to His children throughout the centuries.

First, He instructed Old Testament ministers to build a large tent where His presence could be found. Within the tent, there was a special room with a large golden box where the Spirit of God dwelled. After executing a ton of rituals and regulations, God authorized the main priest to visit the special room once a year, and only that one person could stand in His presence. Later, King Solomon constructed a large, exquisite temple, and the Bible explains God's presence resided in that holy place of worship. Finally, Jesus Christ entered the earth, and for the first time since Adam and Eve, mankind walked and talked with God. Still, that wasn't His closest moment with us.

It wasn't until Jesus left the earth that God came nearer than ever before. God's presence was no longer contained by a box, a building, or even the person of Jesus. Instead, Jesus enthusiastically announced, "I will ask the Father, and he will give you another Advocate, who will never leave you. He is the Holy Spirit, who leads into all truth. The world cannot receive him, because it isn't looking for him and doesn't recognize him. But you know him, because he lives with you now and later will be in you" (John 14:16-17). For the first time in history, the presence of God would now literally reside in the human heart.

The presence of God isn't trapped in a church building or some other sacred location. God's real, noticeable presence remarkably lives in you. It's the most remarkable promise in the Bible. Paul wrote, "Don't you realize that your body is the temple of the Holy Spirit, who lives in you and was given to you by God?" (1 Corinthians 6:19a NLT). When you focus your faith on Jesus, you receive His all-access pass called salvation, and you literally house the very Spirit of God.

What does that mean for us, the rising generation? I honestly think some of us are misinformed about this entire reality. Let me put it to you this way. If Bill Gates was my cousin, and he reminded me daily that if I ever got into a financial jam, all I needed to do was call; if he repeatedly insisted that if I need anything whatsoever, he would unquestionably pay for it, wouldn't it be insane if I constantly complained about not having enough money to eat? Wouldn't it be silly if I rode a bike because I could no longer afford a car payment? I would be a total fool for not taking big Bill up on his promises and not maximizing my access to such a high-powered person.

So many fail to understand the outrageous privilege of gaining total access to God and having the Architect of the universe available to them. It wasn't much different in the days of Moses.

So many fail to understand the outrageous privilege of gaining total access to God and having the Architect of the universe available to them. It wasn't much different in the days of Moses.

You're probably aware of the history. Israel, God's chosen people, fell under the tyranny of Egypt and consequently all became slaves. Day and night they worked tirelessly to build the massive structures that still characterize the ancient empire today. One day, God visited Moses and commissioned him to return to Egypt and break the children of Israel free. Over and over again, Moses boldly petitioned the Egyptian rulers to release the people so they could worship God in the wilderness. After much drama, the people of Israel finally reached the wilderness, and their moment arrived to encounter God in life-changing way.

The creator God pulls the curtain back and shows His glory and presence at the top of a mountain. Instead of racing up the mountain to experience the God of heaven, the people cower back. They stay at the base of the mountain. "You go up for us," they insist to Moses. "You talk to God. You tell us what He wants to say." (See Deuteronomy 5:4-5.) They fail to capitalize on the divine opportunity of complete and total access to God.

Some time later, Moses climbs the mountain a second time. This time, however, he lays out the most audacious request in human history. Look at Moses go.

> Then Moses said to him, If your Presence does not go with us, do not send us up from here. How will anyone know that you are pleased with me and with your people unless you go with us? What else will distinguish me and your people from all the other people on the face of the earth? And the LORD said to Moses. I will do the very thing you have asked, because I am pleased with you and I know you by name.

> Then Moses said, "Now show me your glory." Exodus 33:15-18 (NIV).

No human being ever dared to throw out such a question. Moses requests to see God without any separation or obscurity, in His full glory. You have to remember that the glory of God is the sum total of all that makes God who He is. It is the very weight and full reality of the One that flung the stars in the universe and created the human soul with His wisdom. So, God tells Moses that no one can see Him and still live, but He promises to walk past Him. Moses hides behind a huge rock, and God Almighty unveils Himself to Moses.

I've recently realized two types of Christians exist: the few and the many. The many don't have living encounters with God. Only the few open up their minds and hearts and dare to ask for a moment in His glory. Only the few dare to climb the mountain.

No Scripture paints the picture more clearly than this one: "He made known His ways to Moses, His acts to the children of Israel" (Psalm 103:7 NIV). Can you see the difference? Moses knew God's ways; he knew God's heart. Israel only knew God from a distance; she knew God solely based on what He did or did not do for them. That's where a lot of young Christians live. They know the "acts" of God more than the "ways" of God. When everything is going great, they worship God. When everything is tough, they run away thinking God is not near. Their relationship with God is confined to what they see because they have never gone up the mountain and had a face-to-face encounter. They've never realized that the God of the universe actually lives in them, and they can know Him intimately.

Repeatedly throughout Jesus' life, the Scriptures show Jesus leaving His disciples and going up to the mountains to pray and meet with God. He escapes the noise and the distractions and takes time with His Father. That's why I am encouraging you to escape, so you can elevate. I am challenging you to leave the many and become one of the few. Most of your friends will be content letting your pastor go up the mountain or their parents go up the mountain. It's time for you to start climbing.

Here's how. First, when you decide to spend time with God, do it how He likes it best. This story will demonstrate my point. A few weeks after I graduated college, I led 50 people on a mission trip to Leon, Nicaragua. At the end of the week, I received a surprising phone call. The crusade director called and said, "The president of Nicaragua wants to meet you." At age 21, I was completely floored. I had always dreamed of meeting kings, national presidents and great leaders one day, but I was certain that time would not come until I was 40 or 50 years old. God had other plans.

As I prepared to meet this dignitary, one of his staff members greeted us just outside of his office. She gave me very clear instructions about how to interact with the President. She told me not to speak in English. "Only Spanish," she insisted. You see, I accommodated him, so the President would not have to accommodate me. She made sure I knew to sit only after he was seated and to stand once he stood. She told me to be very complimentary of his people and country. After running through a list of other important protocols, I faced a decision. I could accept her input and operate according to the guidelines she set forth, or I could reject her advice. After all, no one was forcing me to spend my time with him how she described. Really, I had every right to approach him however I wanted. I knew, though, that my time with the President would not be optimal unless I acted in a way that he preferred.

A lot of people carry a certain attitude when they decide to spend time with God. People say, "I want to approach

God my way." It's true. God's given us a free will, so we have every right to approach God however we want. But if we want to maximize our moments with Him, we need to learn what He like best. We need to accommodate Him instead of forcing Him to accommodate us.

The Old Testament contains thousands of extremely detailed rules concerning how God desired Israel to interact with Him. Because of the cross, those rules are now obsolete, but the principles are timeless. Psalms 100:4 NLT says, "Enter his gates with thanksgiving; go into his courts with praise. Give thanks to him and praise his name." The book of Revelation details the mind-blowing atmosphere of heaven. Surrounding the throne for eons of time, angels and beings worship; they bow before the King, and for all of eternity God sits in an environment of wholehearted worship.

One of the most effective ways to approach God in your "journey up the mountain" is to start with praise and worship. That's why the Psalmist said to enter His gates and come into His courts with praise and worship. Some people say, "That's not the way I do it. I don't like to sing to God. I'm the more reserved, reflective type." They cut themselves short of an encounter. Worship prepares the way for God to come close to us.

In high school, I remember coming home some days, turning on a worship album, and just praising God totally alone in my room. Immediately, all of my struggles, insecurities, and issues would melt away. God would invade my bedroom with His power. As a college student, I had the most exciting 4 years with friends and travel, but my most treasured moments are the times of worship I had alone with God.

Today, when you start your prayer time, before you ask God for help or anything else, simply worship. Turn on a worship mix and watch God invade your space. Principle number one for taking advantage of your access to God: find out what God likes and do it.

Here's the next principle to remember that will make your time with God the most incredible part of your day: remind yourself of His character. Sometimes when we come into the presence of God, we feel shameful or down because of mistakes or things going on in our head. Before you jump right into prayer, take a minute and think about who it is you are connecting with. Think about His mercy, His grace, His all-encompassing forgiveness, His unending love. I think about Scriptures like Romans 8:38-39 NLT, "And I am convinced that nothing can ever separate us from God's love. Neither death nor life, neither angels nor demons, neither our fears for today nor our worries about tomorrow – not even the powers of hell can separate us from God's love." As I contemplate His extraordinary love, my shame and reluctance disappear, and I am ready to experience my powerful God.

I even think about God's passion for me. Deuteronomy 4:24 NLT says, "The LORD your God is a devouring fire; He is a jealous God." James 4:5 similarly says, "Or do you think the Scripture says in vain, 'The Spirit who dwells in us yearns jealously?'" (NKJV). Have you ever been jealous of someone? Isn't it the most nagging, unique emotion? That's how God feels about you. The Spirit of God inside of you literally feels a burning jealousy for more of your heart. When I think about that fact, I am ready to pray. I am ready to seek the face of God. Instead of feeling like God is taking time out of His busy schedule to do me a favor, I recognize His eternal, jealous love for me is so vast that He greatly looks forward to my next few minutes with Him. The knowledge of His character fuels my prayer life.

The third timeless principle that will help you in maximizing your time with God is read the Bible. This suggestion might seem extraordinarily elementary to you; however, most Christians I know actually almost never read their Bible. I remember how every, single week I grew up going to church, the Sunday school teachers would ask, "What's the most important way to strengthen your relationship with God?" Everyone would shoot their hands up in the air and scream "Read your Bible!" Even little children knew the principle; however, so few actually open up their Bible and systematically read it.

Instead of feeling like God is taking time out of His busy schedule to do me a favor, I recognize His eternal, jealous love for me is so vast that He greatly looks forward to my next few minutes with Him.

The Bible is the power source to our spiritual life. Books about the Bible are good, but there is nothing more hard-hitting than the actual book. It is loaded with truth, spilling with revelation, and will utterly rock your world. As a freshman in high school, I committed to never go to bed at night without reading at least one chapter. That small commitment did more for me spiritually than a million retreats or conferences. Let me challenge you today to open up your Bible, read through the Gospels, and their the rest of the New Testament. Allow God to talk to you through His book.

The fourth critical principle in catapulting your time with God is relentless passion. Did you ever get sick with a fever and upset stomach? As you lie down, totally weak and exhausted, the first thing you lose is your appetite. Even the thought of food sickens you because when your health leaves, your hunger tends to leave with it. Spiritually, the same thing takes place. When we are healthy spiritually, we are hungry for God. When we are spiritually sick, we lose our hunger and passion for Him. Here's an irrefutable truth: unless you diligently, relentlessly seek after God, you will never experience Him at the top of His mountain. Check this Scripture out: "... he who comes to God must believe that He is, and that He is a rewarder of those who diligently seek Him" (Hebrews 11:6 NKJV). *Diligently* means consistentlyand with intensity. How often do you consistently, intensely seek after God?

Jesus promised in luke 11:9-10 NIV, Ask and it will be given to you; seek and you will find; knock and the door will be opened to you. For everyone who asks receives; he who seeks finds; and to him who knocks, the door will be opened." Those who do not have and do not find and do not get open doors, fail to ask, seek, or knock. Because when you ask, when you seek, when you knock persistently, you will find God every time.

The Psalmist cried out, "O God, you are my God; I earnestly search for you. My soul thirsts for you; my whole body longs for you in this parched and weary land where there is no water. I have seen you in your sanctuary and gazed upon your power and glory. Your unfailing love is better than life itself; how I praise you!" (Psalm 63:1-3 NLT). You can feel the desperation in his voice. His soul poured out a prayer of desperation and passion.

Sometimes you have to get in your car, drive 10 or 20 minutes away from everyone and just spill your guts to the Lord. You have to say to the Lord how much you despise the emptiness of this world and the evil all around you. You have to tell Him how much the material things of this earth and having the praise of man grossly pales in comparison to Him. You have to tell Him how you would rather have Him more than absolutely anything.

A.W. Tozer powerfully prayed in his book *The Pursuit of God*, "O God, I have tasted Thy goodness, and it has both satisfied me and made me thirsty for more. I am painfully conscious of my need of further grace. I am ashamed of my lack of desire. O God, the Triune God, I want Thee; I long to be filled with longing; I thirst to be made more thirsty still. Show me Thy glory, I pray Thee, that so I may know Thee indeed." This perfectly describes how a meeting on the top of the mountain transforms you. It both "satisfies and makes you thirst for more!"

More than our money, our time, and our religious routines, God wants our hearts. The prophet Joel powerfully spoke, "'Even now,' declares the LORD, 'return to me with all your heart, with fasting and weeping and mourning. Rend your heart and not your garments. Return to the LORD your God'" (Joel 2:12-13 NIV). God is far less concerned about the external aspects in our life appearing great. He is focused on our heart. He wants our full attention and allegiance.

How would you like to make your time with God the most extraordinary part of your day? What if you couldn't wait to get home after work or school, so that you could pray? What if worship services became something you craved? What if you were never disappointed after taking time with God? This is what God says, "12 When you call on me, when you come and pray to me, I'll listen. When you come looking for me, you'll find me. Yes, when you get serious about finding me and want it more than anything else, I'll make sure you won't be disappointed" (Jeremiah 29:12-13 MSG). Relentless, passionate pursuit will always keep you in total awe of God and never close to being a disappointment in your spiritual life. Do not say You are too young to seek after God with all your heart, and get a hold of him like few people on the earth.

The last important element to remember when you determine to spend time with God is the "heart check." You quickly realize that clinging to unrepentant sin is nearly impossible if you want to go anywhere in your journey up the mountain. You might have gone somewhere, said something, or thought something, and your conscience screamed at you the entire time. After an internal battle, you may have justified it in your head and carried on. However, when it comes time to pray, that sin will surface. In the presence of the Lord, all things are laid bare. Your compromise will suddenly be impossible to ignore. David cried, "Who may climb the mountain of the LORD? Who may stand in his holy place? Only those whose hands and hearts are pure" (Psalms 24:4 NLT). After you start praying, you'll realize the areas you need to repent, you'll see where your attitude needs to change. This is one of the most powerful times in our meetings with God because it is in these divine instances that God totally transforms us.

In the "heart check" moment, God takes us from weakness and makes us strong. I remember being so frustrated as a teenager over my inconsistency. One week I was blazing, and the next week I was cold. One day I lived the way I wanted to, the next day I was struggling. When I determined to climb up the mountain and meet God, he began to make me the man of God I wanted to become. That's what He does. He fortifies our spirits and alters our desires until we reflect His actual personality.

Each time we ask for forgiveness and cleanse our hearts before God, we take a huge step up the mountain. We actually posture our lives to be touched by Him. The areas of our heart that were hardened, He softens, and that softening enables us to experience Him at a way higher level. The prophet spoke, "...Plow up the hard ground of your hearts, for now is the time to seek the LORD...",(Hosea 10:12 NLT). When we "plow up the hard ground" of our hearts, we actually prime ourselves for an encounter.

> *The areas of our heart that were hardened He softens, and that softenng enables us to experience Him at a way higher level.*

In the book of James, there is a phenomenal promise. James writes, "Come close to God, and God will come close to you. Wash your hands, you sinners; purify your hearts, for your loyalty is divided between God and the world" (James 4:8 NLT). When we purify and cleanse, we come close to God. According to this Scripture, it causes God to draw close to us.

If you will remember to spend time with God with these five things in mind – approach Him the way that He desires, remind yourself of His character, read the Bible, relentlessly seek Him, and always do a heart check – you will be among the few encountering God regularly. You will utilize your all-access pass to God and not let one drop of what Jesus died to give you go to waste.

Are you hungry? Why don't you escape the crowds, turn off your cell phone, close your laptop, even put down this book, and elevate.

9 LISTEN UP

Nearly 7 billion people roam planet earth. Two-thirds or more don't follow Christ. Religions such as Islam, New-Age, Buddhism, Hinduism, and Judaism characterize the core beliefs of so many people across the globe. Every Christ-follower eventually asks themselves the glaring question, "What makes Christianity more than just another religion?" What makes Jesus Christ the truth? What makes our knowledge of God distinct? Without a doubt, the response must be relationship.

Unlike any other religious icon or mainstream belief, Jesus Christ exclusively offers us an unmatched relationship and a tangible connection. No one else and nothing else delivers such a package. Only in Jesus do we receive the promise of a God who constantly cares, forgives, loves, blesses, and most importantly, communicates. Our dynamic relationship with God makes Christianity more than just another religion.

God speaks to us. Imagine that. The uncreated Creator actually takes huge interest in us. The very first human family heard God's voice. In the garden, God called Adam by name. Then sin entered the world, and God still never stopped communicating. From Noah to Abraham, from the prophets to the judges, from the kings to the priests, God spoke powerfully to all of them. God marked every major biblical character's life with a course-altering word. To Abram, He said, "Leave." To Noah, He said "Build." To Moses, He said, "Deliver." To David, He said "Lead." To Paul, He said, "Preach." The trajectory of their entire lives shifted instantaneously after having heard the voice of God.

In the U.S., 95% of people say they are Christians, but we don't often hear about people saying they hear the voice of God. In fact, many believers think that God doesn't speak to us anymore—at least not like He did in the Bible. People who do claim to hear from God are labeled as fakes. They say, "He might have called out to Samuel, but He won't talk to me like that." Why is this? Maybe we've quit listening. Maybe we're not looking for it.

Have you ever heard the voice of God?

I know I have. In most every instance, His clear, gentle voice shook my world. God told me things that didn't make sense in the moment, but as time played out, His remarkable genius shined. Hearing the voice of God has utterly shaped my entire destiny. Without it, I would be lost, miserable, and hopelessly failing.

God wants to speak to us often. Jesus said, "My sheep listen to my voice; I know them and they follow me. I give them eternal life, and they shall never perish; no one can snatch them out of my hand" (John 10:27-28 NIV). To me, this remains one of the most exhilarating promises the Lord ever made. God actually wants to talk with us, and God actually does speak to us. In this passage, Jesus refers to himself as a "shepherd." I think the imagery the Bible uses to help explain the reality of God is so brilliant. A shepherd is effectively married to his sheep. A shepherd expends years standing right beside his flock. He guards, directs, and shields so faithfully that the sheep grow to trust his every word. Jesus said, "My sheep know my voice." In other words, once you've heard the voice of the Lord, its distinctive quality imprints your consciousness. You can clearly distinguish the difference between your own thoughts, the enemy's condemning, tempting words, and the unparalleled voice of the Father.

I'll never forget the season of my life when I went from knowing God speaks to actually hearing God speak. The voice of the Lord brought me to tears on numerous occasions because His voice resonated with a wild amount of love. For the first couple years, most of what God communicated to me centered around my personal relationship with Him. I believe it's because God was establishing a foundation in my walk with Him. When I was 20, I began to hear the voice of God as instructions and very clear directives. He started telling me what to do, where to go, how to do it. It was amazing.

I can confidently say you will experience something similar. In the formative years of your relationship with God, most of what God communicates to you will likely concentrate on your walk with Him. He'll whisper reassuring words, offer gentle correction, and reveal how much you mean to Him. Once your wholehearted love relationship firmly establishes, God typically adds a new layer of communication. You will begin to hear marching orders.

He will entrust you with clear-cut assignments. I like to say it is there the adventure begins.

It was the fall of my senior year in college. I had just finished my first international crusade that summer, and I was still in awe at the entire experience. I knew in 6 short months I would graduate, and my life would begin. Thoughts about my future flooded my consciousness. Would I return home and work on staff at my home church? Would I ask a major evangelist if I could intern for them, so I could be mentored? Would I stay at school and finish my master's degree? I didn't know which path to take. Every option seemed to be a logical next step.

Sitting in the library one afternoon, I struggled to keep my eyes open. Finally, I buried my head into my arms and fell asleep right at a desk for 10 or 15 minutes. As I woke up, I rubbed my eyes and prepared for another stretch of reading when suddenly and unexpectedly, I heard the distinguishable voice of God. "Dominic, you are to do two international crusades this summer. Believe me for 50,000 people to be in attendance at each event and for 100,000 to pay for both outreaches." It was so clearly not my own thoughts that I quickly grabbed a sheet of scrap paper and wrote down precisely what the Lord spoke.

The whole afternoon, I just stared at that piece of paper. 2 crusades, 50,000 people in attendance, $100,000. I was completely flipped out. I couldn't believe God entrusted me with such a considerable assignment. I was flying high and so excited. Then, it dawned on me. Who's going to give $100,000 to a 21-year old? I went from stoked to scared in about 5 seconds. I felt all my excitement drain out like a funnel. I decided to go for a drive.

I jumped in the car and began navigating the city when my cell phone rang. I picked it up, and it was a woman from my father's church. "Dominic, I had a dream last night about you. I felt the Lord telling me that I was supposed to throw you a big party to celebrate your 21st birthday, but more importantly, to celebrate the launch of your worldwide evangelism ministry. Then, I want you to share what God is putting in your heart, and I want to invite people to help you!"

> *If you don't hear from God, your life will be ordinary, unfulfilling and dull. He holds the secrets to everything you could ever dream.*

I was stunned. Hours after the Lord spoke to me, this woman calls and lays out this plan because she had a dream the previous night! Three weeks later the party happened, and to my complete astonishment, the guests contributed more than $30,000 toward the summer campaigns. That began six crazy months. Between God speaking to me every day in the library at ORU and the moment I walked onto the platform in Iquitos, Peru three weeks after graduation, extraordinary miracles happened. Every last penny needed to meet the $100,000 budget came in, all because I listened to our all-knowing Heavenly Father.

If you don't hear from God, your life will be ordinary, unfulfilling and dull. He holds the secrets to everything you could ever dream. He knows how to get you where you need and want to go. He understands you better than anyone, and He knows exactly what to speak to help you every single day.

Without food, your body begins to shut down. Starvation ends thousands of people's lives all over the earth. The body's desperate requirement for food parallels our heart's desperate need for the voice of God. Jesus taught us this truth during His temptation in the wilderness. Near the end of Jesus' forty-day fast, the enemy ruthlessly tempted Christ to turn the stones of the desert into bread. To his temptation, Jesus countered with "People do not live by bread alone, but by every word that comes from the mouth of God" (Matthew 4:4 NLT). In other words, just like your belly needs food, your spirit needs to hear from God. Without it, your spirit weakens.

How does God speak us? In the Bible, we see God speaking in many different ways to his children. You may say, "Well, He's never spoken to me. That kind of thing happened in the Bible, but it doesn't happen much now." Maybe that is just because your expectations of how He speaks may be different from reality. I am going to take a few moments and explain how God speaks, so that you can learn to recognize His voice. A solid understanding of these principles provides a framework for your ability to hear Him.

The first one I call the classic. It's the "still, small voice." People reference this form repeatedly when they say they have heard from God. Very rarely do people hear God with their actual ears. It almost never happens. They do, however, hear with spiritual ears. Constantly, Jesus said, "If anyone has ears, let him hear." The entire crowd had physical ears, but only few knew how to listen with the ears of their spirit. Let's talk about this "still, small voice." The best way for me to describe it is that it doesn't come from your mind; it comes from a deeper place. For me, I sense it from the depths of my heart. It usually shocks my own mind! Even when corrective, the voice of God resonates with love. Even when firm, it is still gentle. Even when surprising, it is still reliable.

Most Bible teachers allude to the story of Elijah when illustrating the way God speaks. God allowed Elijah to experience many dramatic events – a strong wind, an earthquake, a fire – but God's communication to Elijah was hidden in the small, not the big.

> Then He said, "Go out, and stand on the mountain before the LORD." And behold, the LORD passed by, and a great and strong wind tore into the mountains and broke the rocks in pieces before the LORD, but the LORD was not in the wind; and after the wind an earthquake, but the LORD was not in the earthquake; and after the earthquake a fire, but the LORD was not in the fire; and after the fire a still small voice".

1 Kings 19:11-12 NKJV)

Just like Elijah heard God in the small, you will likely hear Him similarly. He may only speak a short phrase or even a word. Don't expect a dramatic discourse, just listen closely to what He says and take note! Literally. It's a good idea to write down what God shows you so you don't forget.

Here's an example of the second major way God speaks.

All throughout high school, I played either the drums or keys in my church's youth group band. In the spring of my senior year, God surprised me. On a Wednesday night, my youth pastor was getting ready to close down his message, so I jumped on the platform and began playing the keys. For five minutes or so, he gave his closing remarks. Then, he abruptly stopped, turned around, pointed his finger at me, and repeated 3 times, "God says develop your character for the next three years, then I will reveal the mystery." What my youth pastor did not know was that for the previous three months, questions about my future bombarded my mind. I knew I had a vision to touch nations with the Gospel, but I didn't know how or when. That night, God spoke through my youth pastor. For the next three years, I diligently worked to build my character and integrity before God. It was exactly three years later that I did my first crusade and the "mystery" of how everything would happen was revealed.

Twelve months later, I had a similar experience when I was attending a conference in Ft. Lauderdale, Florida. I walked up to one of the speakers, Dr. Myles Munroe, and asked him to pray over me. He laid his hands upon me and said, "In 24 months, you will know exactly what you will be doing for the rest of your life." God used Dr. Myles Munroe to confirm the words I heard from my youth pastor. Clearly, God was trying to show me that I was not far from my destiny. Instead, it was just around the corner. Many times, God chooses to speak through people to get a message across to our hearts. Of course, you always have to check everything out with the Scriptures and prayer. If someone tells you they have a message for you from God and it just doesn't seem biblical or you feel uneasy in your heart, you will know it is not from God. Otherwise, listen up!

I remember ministering at a youth retreat in Lancaster, Pennsylvania. Lindsay and I had just finished speaking four times and at the end of the last service, all of the youth came up to pray over us. During the prayer time, a fourteen-year old looked at Lindsay and said, "God is going to use you to help orphans around the world." Lindsay had never even been to an orphanage, let alone felt a calling to help them.

Two weeks later, we were in India doing missions. All throughout the week, Lindsay kept asking me if she could visit an orphanage. At first I ignored the question because our schedule was so packed. Finally she pulled me aside and said, "I want to take the word seriously I received from the teenager in Pennsylvania. How will I be able to help orphans if I have never even seen an orphanage?" I agreed and arranged for the local church pastor to bring her to one while I preached the morning conference.

What she saw changed her life forever. Seventy children packed into a small concrete room, and all of them had walked long distances to come. Lindsay asked where the children slept and the pastor's wife explained they did not have a permanent facility for these orphans. All the children literally came every single day to receive their one meal a day. The pastor's wife explained how it was her dream to one day have a permanent home for these orphaned children. Almost instantly, God spoke to Lindsay's heart and led her to take on the project personally. Today, 50 of those orphans have a brand new home constructed just for them, and Lindsay started an entire rescue orphanage ministry entitled "Angel House." She now has a vision to build 100 orphanages in India alone. Listen up when godly people pray over you. God will often speak through others to get us a message.

How else does God communicate with us? He communicates through impressions. As a kid, I'm sure you experienced this at some point or another. Maybe you said something you shouldn't have or you were picking on your little sister, and your mom gave you "the look." Even though she didn't say a single word, "the look" communicated pages of information. The Bible says, "The spirit of man is the candle of the LORD..." (Proverbs 20:27). God directs us in our spirit and communicates to us without using words sometimes. The Holy Spirit will give us a distinctive feeling, positive or negative, about something. We will know if we should move forward or back away. I'm sure this happened to you before. Maybe you were praying and all of the sudden someone's name came on your heart. You picked up the phone to encourage them and see how they're doing, and your found out that's exactly what they needed. Or, maybe you agreed to go out somewhere with friends, and suddenly a total lack of peace overcame you. It is those nights, when you go anyway, that something negative happened to you or a friend. I can't count the people who have been spared from all kinds of trouble because the Holy Spirit warned them through an impression in their hearts.

Throughout this book, I've referenced the fourth way God speaks – dreams and visions. Mary's husband Joseph was warned in a dream. God spoke to the apostle Paul in dreams. The Old Testament prophets received countless visions. The disciple John experienced a vision of the end times on the Island of Patmos. Clearly, the Bible teaches that God speaks to His children in this way. Remember, if you feel God spoke to you through a dream or a vision, test the dream or vision with God's Word. God will never communicate something to you contrary to the Scriptures. Talk to your pastor or spiritual mentor about your dream or vision and allow them to coach you.

And finally, the most obvious, yet powerful, way God speaks to us is through His written Word. The Bible is God's letter to you. As you read it, the voice of God comes through each page. It never fails. The Scriptures carry the wisdom of God, and He uses them to teach us about Him and about life. He will emphasize different parts each time to speak directly to all the things going on in your life. The people who don't read God's Word miss out on so much. They miss out on one of God's primary methods of communicating to His kids.

The Scriptures carry the wisdom of God, and He uses them to teach us about Him and about life.

Listen up because God's speaking. He's sending you clear messages. Whether in a dream, directly to your heart, throughout His word, or through somebody in your life, He's communicating. He's your Creator, your Father, and your Savior. He's worth listening to.

10 HEAR THE CRY

Certain moments linger in your memory forever, especially when they defy everything that is familiar to you. At 14, I had one of those moments. I was three weeks into a month-long missions adventure in India when a small teenage group and I entered the city of Varanasi, the region I later learned was the actual birthplace of Hinduism and Buddhism. Streaming through the base of the ancient city was a vast, filthy river called Ganges. I slowly walked down the dusty steps leading to the Ganges River and found myself overtaken with the images. To my left, hundreds of people enthusiastically plunged themselves over and over again into the murky water, feverishly bathing. Others actually cupped their hands to the stream to drink, and some sat and waded in the water. To my right, not more than a couple hundred yards off, thick, dark ash cascaded into the river. As I peered closer, I noticed the ashes were from several dead bodies burning on open flames.

Why, I wondered, would anyone drink and bathe in water so riddled with bacteria and disease. I later learned it was the ultimate wish of a Hindu to be cremated along the riverbank of the Ganges because of an ancient belief that spreading their ashes on the "holy river" guarantees them a better position in the next life.

Out from the water emerged an older man who was skinny, wrinkled, and soaking wet with blood smeared on his forehead. (When Hindus go to the temple, often the temple priest will slaughter a goat and smear the blood from the goat on the foreheads of the people.) To this day, I can still see his weathered face and wavy silver hair. Overcome with curiosity, I headed towards him. "Sir!" I exclaimed. "Why are you bathing in that water? Don't you know that it's filled with disease? They're burning bodies and spreading the ashes right here!"

By this time our faces were inches apart and drops of blood were falling from his brow. Next, he said something that shocked me. With pain in his eyes he said, "I am trying to be made clean. I am trying to be made clean. The river can make you clean."

In that instance, it was never clearer that every human being on the planet has a troubled conscience, a real knowledge of sin. Even though that man had never entered a church or heard a preacher explain the concept of redemption, his conscience was marked with guilt and he wanted to be free. What that precious old man had yet to hear was only the river that flowed from Jesus Christ 2,000 years ago could make him clean, not the goat's blood on his forehead from a Hindu temple and certainly not the lifeless, winding river Ganges. That day he heard, and he heard it from a 14 year old.

If you listen closely, you will hear it – a distinct, painful cry sounding from every corner of the globe. It is a cry for love, a cry for freedom, a cry for hope, a cry for answers. From the tiny villages in the African grasslands to the jungles of the Amazon, from the skyscrapers in Hong Kong to the mansions of the rich and famous in the U.S., a cry is pouring out from the hearts of people everywhere. Every child who has just learned of their parents' divorce, every teen who abused drugs for the first time, every orphan who lacks food and water, every individual suffering without the knowledge and understanding of God, they all hang in the balance of eternity.

Eternity. How often do you think about it? Do you ever think about life after your lungs stop breathing and your heart stops pumping? It's amazing how little it crosses people's minds considering how massive a reality it is. Eternity means unending. It means forever. The Bible says "God has made everything beautiful for its own time. He has planted eternity in the human heart..." (Ecclesiastes 3:11 NLT). Death feels unnatural and foreign to us because God instilled a sense of eternity in the heart of every person. In the center of our consciousness, we know our lives constitute more than living 80 or 90 years on this planet, then ceasing to exist. We know we have an eternal nature.

At the very end of Jesus' time as man on this earth, He carefully selected the final words he would deliver. He gave us a sneak preview of the end of the age. He provided a stunning picture of what will transpire when the world, as we know it, ends. Check these verses out:

When the Son of Man comes in his glory, and all the angels with him, he will sit on his throne in heavenly glory. All the nations will be gathered before him, and he will separate the people one from another as a shepherd separates the sheep from the goats. He will put the sheep on his right and the goats on his left. "Then the King will say to those on his right, "Come, you who are blessed by my Father; take your inheritance, the kingdom prepared for you since the creation of the world. For I was hungry and you gave me something to eat, I was thirsty and you gave me something to drink, I was a stranger and you invited me in, I needed clothes and you clothed me, I was sick and you looked after me, I was in prison and you came to visit me.

Then the righteous will answer him, Lord, when did we see you hungry and feed you, or thirsty and give you something to drink? When did we see you a stranger and invite you in, or needing clothes and clothe you? When did we see you sick or in prison and go to visit you?

The King will reply, 'I tell you the truth, whatever you did for one of the least of these brothers of mine, you did for me.

Then he will say to those on his left, Depart from me, you who are cursed, into the eternal fire prepared for the devil and his angels. For I was hungry and you gave me nothing to eat, I was thirsty and you gave me nothing to drink, I was a stranger and you did not invite me in, I needed clothes and you did not clothe me, I was sick and in prison and you did not look after me.

They also will answer, Lord, when did we see you hungry or thirsty or a stranger or needing clothes or sick or in prison, and did not help you?

He will reply, I tell you the truth, whatever you did not do for one of the least of these, you did not do for me.' "Then they will go away to eternal punishment, but the righteous to eternal life.

Matthew 25:31-46 NIV

He says that "all of the nations" will stand before him. Imagine billions of people, literally the entire human race, standing before the Lord. Then, Jesus explains, a massive divide occurs, and the entire mass of humanity is split down the middle. One group of people forcibly shifts to the right and the other to the left until you have two distinct groups of people, separated in a very real way. The division between these groups in no way reflects the divisions of the present day: young or old, rich or poor, American or European, African or Latin. The difference rests singularly on one thing – whether or not they reached out to the hurting, the lost and the suffering throughout their lifetime.

The passage further explains on that final day that Jesus will sit on his throne as the great judge and King. We don't always envision Jesus like this. We envision Him smiling, holding children, maybe healing the sick. In that day, He will exercise the divine authority the Father granted Him; He will be King Jesus. Then, He compares His actions to a shepherd separating sheep and goats. (In the Ancient Mid-East, shepherds used to peel through their flocks and divide out the sheep from the goats. The sheep were of much greater value and usually set off to the side.) Jesus vows to divide the people of the earth in the same way. The sheep will be those who have compassionately responded to the cry of the broken and suffering, and the goats are those who ignored it or just made excuses. The goats are those who probably had good intentions, but never ended up turning those intentions into tangible help for the broken. He ends his talk by warning everyone that the sheep enter eternity in heaven, but the goats are forced into punishment (in hell).

What I have discovered is that there are two very real cries in the world. The first cry is the cry of the poor, the broken, and the hurting. Here's how it usually goes. Whether it's a news headline you caught while you were flipping through the channels or a shocking story you heard from a close friend, when you hear it, you might shake your head in doubt or even well up with frustration. The first cry may even cause you to tear up or give you goose bumps. But at the end of the day, when people hear this cry, they typically go on with their lives and business as usual. Little, if anything, changes. Have you ever heard this type of cry? Maybe you've seen a commercial on TV or heard a missionary speak at your church and felt sorrow for the people involved. However, as soon as the program was finished or you walked out of the building, the impact was gone. I am sure this has happened to many of us at some point.

The second cry is totally different because it shakes you to your core. It reverberates in your heart for years, and you are incapable of living life the same way after hearing it. This second cry is the cry that comes from God to us. It's the cry of God to His sons and daughters to rise up and do something. A certain man heard this cry, and it forever rocked his world. His name was Isaiah. Isaiah was uniquely granted a non-stop ticket to the throne room of God, the very room where God lives. God's room is an absolutely wild place. There are all kinds of stunning noises and beings and worship songs coming from this room, and there's no place in the created world that comes close to it. Here's what Isaiah heard and saw:

In the year that King Uzziah died, I saw the Lord seated on a throne, high and exalted, and the train of his robe filled the temple. Above him were seraphs, each with six wings: With two wings they covered their faces, with two they covered their feet, and with two they were flying. And they were calling to one another: "Holy, holy, holy is the LORD Almighty; the whole earth is full of his glory." At the sound of their voices the doorposts and thresholds shook and the temple was filled with smoke

Then I heard the voice of the Lord saying, "Whom shall I send? And who will go for us?" And I said, "Here am I. Send me!"

Isaiah 6:1-4,8 NIV

Isaiah saw God Almighty in His room, on His heavenly throne. Of all the things God could communicate, He lifts up His voice and says, "Whom shall I send? Who will go?" I imagine that loud cry pierced through the atmosphere of heaven and that every being was silenced as the holy, uncreated God laid down that weighty question. Isaiah, moved and convicted, humbly lifts his head and says, "Here am I. Send me."

I believe that very same cry spills from the heart of God toward us today but with an even greater intensity. In fact, I believe God is shouting it over our generation. He's crying, "Whom shall I send? Who will go?" It's echoing across the world to His sons and daughters. Can you hear it? Once you hear it, you won't be able to ignore it. You won't be able to sit still, and you certainly won't be able to remain silent.

One day, the disciples ran up to Jesus and asked Him about his lunch plans. Jesus totally ignored their question and passionately said, "Do not say there are four more months. Lift up your eyes! The harvest is white!" (John 4:35). One of the students from my college dorm grew up on a farm. One day he described, in vivid detail, what a "white harvest" looks like. He said when the harvest is white, there is absolutely nothing like it. As far as your eyes can see, the white crops just blow in the wind, but you have to be careful. If the white crops are not picked and harvested in time, they will fall to the ground and die. It's the final point of the crop's readiness.

Jesus likened those ripe crops to the broken and hurting people all around us. When Jesus said, "Disciples! Lift up your eyes," He was really communicating, "see the world like I see it! The way you write people off and consider them spiritually hopeless is wrong!" Every single human being, regardless of his or her religious background, family life, nationality, color, or income is totally ready for a life-altering encounter with God. Stop saying "Four more months!" Stop thinking next time or next year will be a better time. Your friends, your neighbors, your co-workers, your relatives are as ready as they will ever be to experience salvation and a miracle life.

One of the most striking passages in the entire New Testament is when Paul said, "But this I say, brethren, the time is short, so that from now on even those who have wives should be as though they had none, those who weep as though they did not weep, those who rejoice as though they did not rejoice, those who buy as though they did not possess, and those who use this world as not misusing it. For the form of this world is passing away" (1 Corinthians 7:29-31 NKIV). What was he saying? Nothing is as it was anymore. The game has changed. We can't just carry on and follow the normal patterns of life - find a spouse, get married, have some hard times, have some good times, buy some cool stuff, and that's it. Everything is different, and the cycles and routines are irrelevant. Everything we used to define our lives by – our possessions, friend list on facebook, hobbies – is about to vanish. It's "passing away." Open up your ears! Hear the piercing cry of God to go to the hurting, the suffering, and the broken.

> *Everything we used to define our lives by – our possessions, friend list on facebook, hobbies – is about to vanish. It's "passing away."*

24 year-old Alex heard the cry.

Alex grew up in a family of 32. His father married 13 women, and he was the child of his father's 13th wife. His father's numerous marriages and divorces produced a staggering 29 brothers and sisters for Alex. At some point in his life, Alex became his father's favorite. The attention and favoritism he received angered his other siblings. Not long after, his father was killed in a car accident. When his dad left the earth, Alex felt utterly and completely alone because all his other family relationships were strained.

One day Alex heard the message about Jesus Christ and he committed his life to God, making him a first-generation Christian. His entire life was cleansed and revolutionized, so he responded to the call of God to go and be a missionary. At 24, he found himself in Nigeria, Africa's most heavily populated nation. Nigeria is a country that is ruled by a Muslim dictator, and for years, there has been political unrest and constant turmoil.

One area overcome by guerilla warriors, grew particularly infamous for kidnapping foreigners and holding them hostage for media attention and money. The guerilla movement initially started out as a group of young people from a university trying to be corrective agents for injustice. Ultimately, however, they became corrupt themselves and began multiplying the injustice. Their constituency grew to over 3,000 strong, and they became exceedingly wealthy by controlling 20% of the entire nation's oil production (the oil industry dominates 80% of Nigeria's economy). Through the black market they sold the oil and secured profits in the billions of dollars. With the money, they purchased the most modern armarment, grenade launchers and guns. The Nigerian government tried to contain them by sending in troops, but the guerillas captured the troops and held the soldiers hostage. The government failed to create a solution for containing the growing problem the guerillas were becoming.

In a place of prayer, God began speaking to Alex's heart. God told Alex, "I want you to pray and get My heart for these guerillas." As Alex listened, God began to reveal His heart for these militants who had been in the jungle for more than 10 years. Alex and 25 other young missionaries (all between the ages of 18-24) began to experience the Holy Spirit breaking their hearts for these unreached people. These militants were so darkened, many turned to the occult to increase their "power." Soon, God began to specifically speak to Alex and the other missionaries. They clearly heard the voice of God saying, "I want you to go and I want you to proclaim."

Alex and the team approached the leadership at Youth With a Mission (YWAM), the mission's organization that sent them to Africa, and began sharing what God was leading them to do. Their leaders heavily questioned them, tested them, and warned them that they could die attempting to reach these militants. Each one still responded with unwavering conviction that they had to go, regardless of the obvious risks at hand. After much prayer, the leadership released them to go.

Immediately, the young team went to guerilla camps asking if they could serve them. They offered to clean up the camp and work for free for several hours a day. "All we ask," they said, "is that we can share something with you after."

There were two specific leaders in the camp who carried

significant influence. Each of them would submit themselves regularly to the power of Satan and go into a "trance." When one would become demonized, he would walk around on all fours like an alligator or a crocodile. When the other would fall into his trance, an insatiable to desire to murder filled his soul.

One afternoon, the second leader fell into his trance. The rest of the militants rushed over to the young team and screamed, "Run! He has to kill! He has to kill!" The militants were actually trying to save the missionaries because over time they had begun to appreciate them. Instead of walking away from the man, Alex began to walk towards him and said "Jesus is going to set him free today!"

Finally, the demonized leader himself began to yell "Run, run, I have to kill you."

Alex quickly responded, "No you don't! Jesus is going to set you free!" The man fell on his knees, dropped his knife, and began to weep. Shortly after, he gave his life to Jesus.

This miraculous moment brought 300 other militants in that area to Christ. Soon, another 600 more came to Christ! Astonishingly, they began to turn all their arms over to the young group of missionaries by the truck loads. When the YWAM group brought the trucks to the police, they asked the police what they should do with these 900 people. The government promised to give them amnesty if the young group would "rehabilitate" them. All of this happened in September 2009 because one young man heard the cry.

Somewhere in the deep jungles of Peru, in the Islamic

Middle East, in Hindu India, in your public high school hallway, in your part-time job, maybe even in your own family, people wait. They're waiting for you. God is waiting for you. Hear the cry, "Who can I send and who will go?" With everything within us, let's say, "Here am I. Send me."

11 BATTLE SCARS

You probably have at least one scar somewhere on your body, and I bet you can remember exactly the moment it happened. It might be from falling off of your bike when you were little, cutting yourself shaving, getting injured during a sport, or even from having a major surgery. Each of those experiences, no matter how great or small, usually marks your memories forever. Every scar tells a story.

"From now on let no one trouble me, for I bear in my body the marks of the Lord Jesus" (Galatians 6:17 NKJV). This is how the great Apostle Paul signed off his letter to the Galatian believers. I am sure these potent words hit pretty hard as they contemplated the full gravity of what he was communicating. Without a doubt, he was alluding to the battle scars scattered across his skin from beatings and scourging. Visible proof of his faithfulness to God actually covered his body.

It's no shock why Paul would tell Timothy, a rising leader in the next generation to "endure hardship as a good soldier." Paul knew from first-hand experience the price of following Christ with wholehearted commitment. He and his band of diehard friends moved in and out of some insane hardships. In 2 Corinthians 4:8-9 NIV he described it by saying, "We are hard pressed on every side, but not crushed; perplexed, but not in despair; persecuted, but not abandoned; struck down, but not destroyed."

Somehow, even in the dark moments, Paul and his band of followers found themselves to be unconquerable. Every time they were attacked, they reemerged stronger and more fortified. They could not be contained or inhibited. Read carefully in these next few pages. I am about to give you a key that the rising generation must grab onto.

I'll never forget the unique experience that transpired on my wedding day. John Bevere, an incredible leader, mentor, and friend, graciously decided to officiate the wedding ceremony. In order to make it to the ceremony in Kansas City on time, he had to fly by private jet through the night after speaking in Canada at a large youth convention. One hour before the ceremony began, we received a call from John explaining how it was utterly impossible for him to come to Kansas City. The pilot insisted it was far too dangerous to proceed any further than St. Louis due to a massive thunderstorm that surrounded the city. The pilot described it like a 30,000-foot vertical wall that was virtually impenetrable. Frustrated, John called my father-in-law and delivered the upsetting news that they were grounded, and there's no way they could make it on time. John's next call was to his wife Lisa. As he began explaining the dramatic weather situation, Lisa began speaking in faith regarding the dilemma. She resolutely prayed for an opening to appear in the weather system. Her faith began to stir John's faith, and they joined their hearts trusting God for a quick answer.

Just a few minutes later, John's pilot called him and said, "You're never going to believe this. A tiny opening emerged in the weather system. I am confident we can make it through!" John hurried back to the airport and headed to Kansas City for the wedding.

When the moment came during the ceremony for the address to the bride and groom, John looked intently at Lindsay and I and began to share from his heart. "Dominic and Lindsay, the Holy Spirit spoke to me while I was driving from the Kansas City airport to the church. He told me that He allowed me to go through the delay because it is a prophetic image of the next season of your lives together." I wasn't really following where he was going. All I knew was that this was the moment I waited my entire life to enjoy. So, I was certain he was about to give me some massive encouraging prophecy like "you've been faithful with little, now God will make you faithful over much!" Or, "today God honors you before this assembly of people. Prepare yourself for unprecedented blessing!"

I smiled and continued listening. "The Lord told me that you and Lindsay are about to come into incredible storms. The storms will be so severe they will appear to be impenetrable every single time." Hmmm. Did he just say that on my wedding day? I must be misunderstanding where he's going. He continued, "In this next season together, you and Lindsay are going to experience incredible trials. Hebrews 5:8 says Jesus learned obedience by the things He suffered." Wow. Ok.

Up to that point, I always saw battles and storms as negatives. I liked to breeze through the parts of the Bible that describe suffering and hardship, especially for the early church. I preferred to study other aspects of the Scriptures, so John's words to me were a great shock.

Then John continued, "The Lord told me that just like it required Lisa's faith to stir my faith to get me here today, so it will be with you and Lindsay. When it looks dark and impossible, you both will join your faith in prayer. At the very last second, you will find a sliver-sized opening in the storms, and you will come through every time."

What I didn't understand on my wedding day was that when you participate in the suffering and "dying" aspect of being a wholehearted follower of Christ, something remarkable follows. That is resurrection.

Paul prayed a pretty wild prayer in Philippians 3:10-11. He said, "I want to know Christ and the power of his resurrection and the fellowship of sharing in his sufferings, becoming like him in his death, and so, somehow, to attain to the resurrection from the dead"(NIV). If you ask most people, "Do you want to know you God?" They'll shout "Yes!" If you ask them, Do you want to experience His power? "They'll shout "yes!" But if you ask, "do you want to fellowship with Jesus in His suffering? Do you want to become like Him in His death?" I doubt you'll see anyone standing on their chair for that one.

What I didn't understand on my wedding day was that when you participate in the suffering and "dying" aspect of being a wholehearted follower of Christ, something remarkable follows. That is resurrection.

One thing is certain. When John Bevere issued the loaded statement regarding the upcoming season and the very difficult moment in our journey forthcoming, truer words had rarely been spoken. One daunting trial after another flooded our lives. Life-long relationships turned on us. People spoke against us. Lies and all sorts of unexpected friction emerged. Things grew extremely challenging, but literally every single time we bounced back stronger.

While we were dying and joining in Christ's sufferings, His resurrection life was overtaking us. I can promise you a few things. When you decide to press into your walk with God while you're still young, you will experience some "dying." I am certainly not referring to physical death, but death to your self and selfishness. When you decide to walk with God, often you walk alone. As a young man, Moses had to make the decision. Was he going to coast through life and miss his destiny? Or, was he going to swallow a serious dose of hardship and fulfill his calling?

Check this out. "By faith Moses, when he had grown up, refused to be known as the son of Pharaoh's daughter. He chose to be mistreated along with the people of God rather than to enjoy the pleasures of sin for a short time. He regarded disgrace for the sake of Christ as of greater value than the treasures of Egypt, because he was looking ahead to his reward" (Hebrews 11:24-26 NIV). As a young person who's running after the heart of God, internalize this verse. Choose "disgrace for the sake of Christ" over acceptance and popularity if necessary. It may not produce the short-term "pleasure" sin guarantees; however, the "reward" is something to which nothing can be compared.

What is the reward? Why would Paul actually pray to know Christ in His suffering? What did the marks on His body really produce in His life? Watch this. Those battle scars provided him the ability to announce, "I have been crucified with Christ and I no longer live, but Christ lives in me. The life I live in the body, I live by faith in the Son of God, who loved me and gave himself for me" (Galatians 2:20 NIV). The moment actually came in Paul's life when he could unequivocally say that when people saw him that didn't see Paul anymore. Christ literally shone through every part of who he had become.

This should be our goal. Now, I find myself praying the entire prayer Paul prayed in front of the Phillipian church. I really want to know God, His power, and His sufferings because as painful and difficult as they are, I am addicted to the resurrection moment. Every single time the heat gets laid on thick and opposition emerges, God does a new work in me and miracles begin taking place. I realize all over again how weak and powerless I am, and how desperately I need Christ. I lean on God at a higher level, and it keeps me broken.

Do you have any "battle scars," definitive moments in your history with God when you took heat for following Jesus? Every scar has a story, and God will use yours to shine through to our world.

12 INSTEAD BE THE EXAMPLE

Some people operate like thermostats, and other people operate like thermometers. The thermostats set the spiritual temperature for the people around them, while the thermometers simply adapt to what's already there. The thermostats create the spiritual atmosphere with their example. Some lead, some follow. Some people are game changers, and some just play the game. Who are you?

Roger Bannister's story reverberates with this truth because Bannister changed the game. Nobody thought running the mile in less than four minutes could be accomplished. Even medical doctors insisted that if an individual attempted to run the mile in under four minutes, the human heart would explode. Every Olympic runner was told it was impossible because no had ever done it. Bannister begged to differ, and on May 6, 1954, he defied the odds and stunned the world when he crossed the finish line in 3 minutes 59 seconds. Bannister's accomplishment inspired runners around the world. In fact, just 46 days later on June 21, Australian John Landy defeated the 4-minute barrier as well. Bannister set the pace, and everyone else followed. Since that year, hundreds matched his record.

I'm learning that when one person does something impossible, everyone else falls in line. Paul basically tells Timothy the same thing. He warns, "Don't let anyone look down on you because you are young, but set an example for all the believers in speech, in life, in love, in faith, and in purity" (1 Timothy 4:12 NIV). He's telling Timothy, 'I know you're young, but don't let anyone put you in a box. Don't let anyone cap your ability. Do the impossible, set the pace, and be the example. Once you've done what no one else has done, once you've lived like no one else has lived, everyone is going to follow you.' In fact, he said the entire church would follow him.

It's time for our parents, our teachers, our pastors, our politicians, and the "respectable" people in our society to take serious note of the rising generation. It's time for them to see us and think, *Wow I have to get my act together. Did you see how they pray and miracles take place? Did you see the standard of purity they live by? Did you see what they're accomplishing for God... at that age?* It's time for us to change the game. Paul told young Timothy "instead, be an example." Why did he say "instead?" He said "instead" because there is an alternative. The alternative is that we continue to live spiritual lives that are crammed in the box. We attend church, go to school, work, and walk around like clones. No one ever breaks out and does anything earth-shattering.

It's time to get some people nervous. It's time to shake some things up. It's time to tire ourselves from the ridiculously stupid norms of our generation: drinking, pre-marital sex, and drug abuse. Someone has to tap into some God-sized power. Someone needs to recognize who they really are and what they are capable of with God. Someone needs to awaken from the "entertainment coma" of movies, music, Internet, and video games that continue to distract and seduce our generation. They temporarily thrill us, but they don't satisfy us. Someone is going to have to get disgusted at the short-lived rush and start asking God for something big.

What are we waiting for? Our parent's generation has done their thing. Now there's a gap. There's an opening for the next group to step up to the plate.

Who's going to hold a school-wide assembly?

Who's going to bring their entire family to Christ?

Who's going to give a million dollars to God's work before they're 30?

Who's going to take Jesus to work with them instead of shuddering with intimidation?

Who's going to be the thermostat?

Who's going to cry out to God in prayer until literal miracles start happening?

Who's going to lead a million people to Christ?

Who's going to turn a university upside down with the reality of God?

Who?

I believe it just takes one. One inspired, bold, uncompromising, fiery young person.

How will our generation see the power and love of Jesus if they don't see it through you? Jesus said as He is, so are we in this world" (1 John 4:17b). What was Jesus like in this world? He split history in two and touched individuals and cities alike. He performed miracles. He connected with people like no had ever witnessed. The Scripture says we are like Him. God doesn't want to hold us back from living powerful lives; He wants to push us forward. He said, "In the same way, let your good deeds shine out for all to see, so that everyone will praise your heavenly Father" Matthew 5:16 NLT). He said, "This is to my Father's glory, that you bear much fruit, showing yourselves to be my disciples" (John 15:8 NIV). More good deeds and more amazing fruit translate into more of God's fame spreading throughout the world because your life embodies Him on the earth.

We need to grow increasingly agitated with our present apathy. We need to grow sickened by the spiritual climate of our youth groups, college ministries, and friends. We need to spark a movement that is uncontainable and viral. John the Baptist said, "I baptize you with water; but someone is coming soon who is greater than I am—so much greater that I'm not even worthy to be his slave and untie the straps of his sandals. He will baptize you with the Holy Spirit and with fire" (Luke 3:16NLT). Fire is dangerous because it's difficult to contain. When a fire is glowing, everyone knows it. It's impossible to ignore because of the effect it produces. It will burn virtually anything in its path. You can feel its heat from the moment it sparks. John spoke prophetically when He spoke about the fire baptism. He knew the day was soon coming when Christ followers would be lit with fire, and their fire would not be politically correct or culturally sensitive.

Jesus cried, "I have come to bring fire on the earth and how I wish it were already kindled!" (Luke 12:49 NIV). He continued by describing what the fire would do. He said, "Do you think I have come to bring peace to the earth? No, I have come to divide people against each other! From now on families will be split apart, three in favor of me, and two against—or two in favor and three against" (Luke 12:51-52). He basically promises that a life baptized in fire creates strained relationships. Of course, not all families and friendships will be strained because God will place powerful men and women around you. Sometimes, however, the people closest to you begin rejecting you when you decide to blaze with fire and be the example. Your fire discomforts them because they've grown to accept mediocrity.

I wonder if there's a David reading this text who is ready to chase a giant while all the other "people of God" cower with fear. I'm curious if there's a Moses who's been running from his destiny, but is ready to square up with God and go deliver his generation. God's peering down from heaven looking for another Joshua and Caleb who have faith in His Word while everyone else discounts His abilities. God's waiting for another Mary who will say "be unto me according to your will" when it costs them their reputation.

At 12 years old, Jesus said, "I must be about my Father's business." He knew who He was and precisely where He was going. He stunned the religious leaders by His wisdom and grasp of the Scriptures. There must be another 12-year old that God's already touched so profoundly they hunger for truth and diligently study the Bible; they understand who they are and what the purposes of God are. Where is the next 17-year old passionately worshipping God behind closed doors while no one watches like David with his flock? When Samuel came to anoint the next leader, he passed by the "older" siblings and landed on the youngest because God accepts heart over skill. He'd rather have brokenness than experience. He'd rather have willingness and passion than genius. As the prophet said, God is searching for a man after his own heart! see (1 Samuel 13:14.)

Listen up. When our heart meets God's heart in secret, He opens doors in public. (See Matthew 6). Seemingly locked, barred, nailed shut doors will swing open for you. When we intimately know our God now, He positions us for greatness later. You may not see it now, but trust in His promises. He declares, "...but the people who know their God shall be strong, and carry out great exploits" (Daniel 11:32 NKJV). Who's going to grab hold of God's heart and know Him like few others know Him? Who's going to trade an unrighteous

> *When we intimately know our God now, He positions us for greatness later.*

dating relationship (the kind you know you shouldn't be in) for a passion to wait for God's time. Who's going to lay down an addictive online habit that's destructive? Who's going to pray and fast while everyone else feeds the media dependency?

It's your time to stand up and be the example. Who's going to lead if not you? If you sit and if you choose only to follow, you will short change your destiny. What are you waiting for? Your generation is waiting for you.

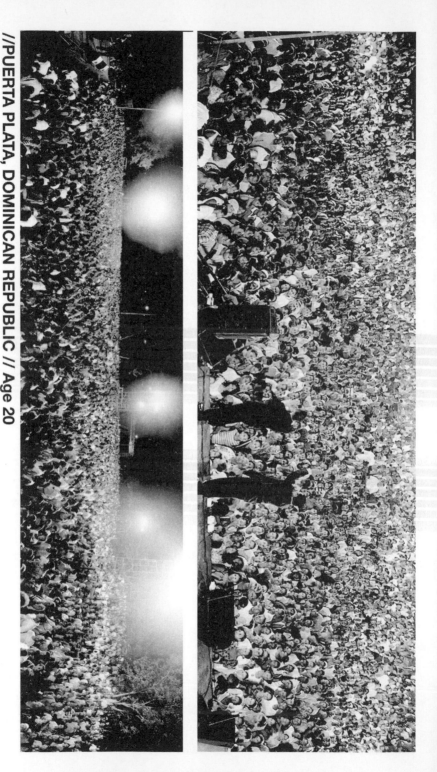

//PUERTA PLATA, DOMINICAN REPUBLIC // Age 20

Dominic's first international campaign.

//LEON, NICARAGUA // Age 21
Dominic meets and prays with President Enrique Bolanos of Nicaragua.

//CAP-HAITIEN, HAITI // Age 23

One of DRM's favorite campaigns in the center of Haiti's 2nd largest city. The people completely packed out the square to the point of overflow.

//BELO HORIZONTE, BRAZIL // Age 22
Over 30,000 gather in the heart of one of Brazil's largest cities and overwhelmingly respond to the gospel.

//MANAGUA, NICARAGUA // Age 25
The DRM missions team fills the stage a few hours before the national campaign begins.

//MANAGUA, NICARAGUA // Age 25
John Bevere leads the pastors conference where over 3,000 pastors from around the city united for an unforgettable conference.

//KURNOOL, INDIA // Age 26

Dominic and Lindsay dedicate churches and wells built by DRM and partners. Bottom right: Lindsay hands food to the Angelhouse orphans. The orphanage houses 50 children full time.

PRAYER OF SALVATION

God loves you--no matter who you are, no matter what your past. God loves you so much that He gave His one and only begotten Son for you. The Bible tells us that "...whoever believes in him shall not perish but have eternal life" (John 3:16 NIV). Jesus laid down His life and rose again so that we could spend eternity with Him in heaven and experience His absolute best on earth. If you would like to receive Jesus into your life, say the following prayer out loud and mean it from your heart.

Heavenly Father, I come to You admitting that I am a sinner. Right now, I choose to turn away from sin, and I ask You to cleanse me of all unrighteousness. I believe that Your Son, Jesus, died on the cross to take away my sins. I also believe that He rose again from the dead so that I might be forgiven of my sins and made righteous through faith in Him. I call upon the name of Jesus Christ to be the Savior and Lord of my life. Jesus, I choose to follow You and ask that You fill me with the power of the Holy Spirit. I declare that right now I am a child of God. I am free from sin and full of the righteousness of God. I am saved in Jesus' name. Amen.

If you prayed this prayer to receive Jesus Christ as your Savior for the first time, please contact us on the web at www.harrisonhouse.com to receive a free book.

Or you may write to us at

Harrison House
P.O. Box 35035
Tulsa, Oklahoma 74153

angel HOUSE

BECAUSE **every** CHILD DESERVES A SAFE PLACE TO CALL **home**

HOW TO help:

1. Go to www.angelhouse.me and click "donate now" to help complete and support the rescue orphanage building program.

2. Spread the word! Become a fan of Angel House on Facebook and follow us on Twitter for updates @theangelhouse

3. Tell your local businesses, schools and churches to contact us for more info on fundraising efforts at info@angelhouse.me

VISIT missions.me
2 JOIN US on a LIFE CHANGING MISSIONS EXPERIENCE